ANTIQUITIES OF
THE MESA VERDE NATIONAL PARK

LECTOR HOUSE PUBLIC DOMAIN WORKS

This book is a result of an effort made by Lector House towards making a contribution to the preservation and repair of original classic literature. The original text is in the public domain in the United States of America, and possibly other countries depending upon their specific copyright laws.

In an attempt to preserve, improve and recreate the original content, certain conventional norms with regard to typographical mistakes, hyphenations, punctuations and/or other related subject matters, have been corrected upon our consideration. However, few such imperfections might not have been rectified as they were inherited and preserved from the original content to maintain the authenticity and construct, relevant to the work. The work might contain a few prior copyright references which have been retained, wherever considered relevant to the part of the construct. We believe that this work holds historical, cultural and/or intellectual importance in the literary works community, therefore despite the oddities, we accounted the work for print as a part of our continuing effort towards preservation of literary work and our contribution towards the development of the society as a whole, driven by our beliefs.

We are grateful to our readers for putting their faith in us and accepting our imperfections with regard to preservation of the historical content. We shall strive hard to meet up to the expectations to improve further to provide an enriching reading experience.

Though, we conduct extensive research in ascertaining the status of copyright before redeveloping a version of the content, in rare cases, a classic work might be incorrectly marked as not-in-copyright. In such cases, if you are the copyright holder, then kindly contact us or write to us, and we shall get back to you with an immediate course of action.

HAPPY READING!

ANTIQUITIES OF THE MESA VERDE NATIONAL PARK

JESSE WALTER FEWKES

ISBN: 978-93-5420-077-9

Published: 1911

LECTOR HOUSE LLP
E-MAIL: lectorpublishing@gmail.com

SMITHSONIAN INSTITUTION
BUREAU OF AMERICAN ETHNOLOGY
BULLETIN 51

ANTIQUITIES OF THE MESA VERDE NATIONAL PARK

CLIFF PALACE

BY

JESSE WALTER FEWKES

1911

LETTER OF TRANSMITTAL

Smithsonian Institution,
Bureau of American Ethnology,
Washington, D. C., May 14, 1910.

Sir: I have the honor to submit the accompanying manuscript, entitled "Antiquities of the Mesa Verde National Park: Cliff Palace," by Dr. Jesse Walter Fewkes, with the recommendation that it be published, subject to your approval, as Bulletin 51 of this Bureau.

Yours, very respectfully,
F. W. Hodge,
Ethnologist in Charge.

Dr. Charles D. Walcott,
Secretary of the Smithsonian Institution,
Washington, D. C.

CONTENTS

LIST OF PLATES

Page

LIST OF FIGURES

CLIFF PALACE, FROM THE SPEAKER-CHIEF'S HOUSE TO THE SOUTH-ERN END.

PHOTOGRAPHED BY F. K. VREELAND.

(Enlarged - Left)

(Enlarged - Right)

INTRODUCTION

In the summer of 1909 the writer was detailed by the Secretary of the Smithsonian Institution, at the request of the Secretary of the Interior, to continue the excavation and repair of ruins in the Mesa Verde National Park, Colorado. This work was placed under his sole charge and continued through the months May to August, inclusive. In that time the writer was able to repair completely this great ruin and to leave it in such condition that tourists and students visiting it may learn much more about cliff-dwellings than was possible before the work was undertaken.

The force of laborers, numbering on an average 15 workmen, was from Mancos, Colorado. Many of them had worked on Spruce-tree House during the previous year and had become expert in repairing ruins. By their aid it was possible to accomplish more and at less expense than was expected. It has fallen to the writer to prepare the report on the work which he had the honor to direct, and he is conscious how difficult it is to put it into a form that will adequately express the devotion with which those under him have accomplished their respective tasks.

A report on the general results accomplished at Cliff Palace was published by the Secretary of the Interior in 1909; the following account considers in a more detailed way the various scientific phases. The purpose of the present paper is to present a more accurate account of Cliff Palace than was possible before the excavation and repair work was done, and to increase existing knowledge by directing attention to the scientific data revealed by excavations of this largest, most picturesque, and most typical cliff-dwelling in the Southwest. In order to give this account a monographic form there have been introduced the most important descriptions of Cliff Palace previously published. There is also included a description of the few minor antiquities brought to light in the progress of the work. These specimens are now in the United States National Museum, where they form the nucleus of a collection from Cliff Palace. The increasing interest, local and national, in the prehistoric culture of the Southwest and the influence of these antiquities in attracting visitors to localities where they exist, furnish a reason for considering in some detail various other questions of general interest connected with cliff-dwellings that naturally suggest themselves to those interested in the history of man in America.

The method of work in this undertaking has been outlined in the report on Spruce-tree House published by the Secretary of the Interior.[1] The primary thought has been to increase the educational value of Cliff Palace by attracting

---

[1] In his Annual Report for 1908. See also *Bulletin 41 of the Bureau of American Ethnology*.

tourists and students of archeology.

The reader is reminded that from the nature of the work at Cliff Palace very few specimens can be expected from it in the future, and that so far as the minor antiquities are concerned the objective material from this ruin is now all deposited in public museums or in private collections. Additional specimens can be obtained, however, from other ruins near it which will throw light on the culture of Cliff Palace. It is appropriate, therefore, to point out, at the very threshold of our consideration, that a continuation of archeological work in the Mesa Verde National Park is desirable, as it will add to our knowledge of the character of prehistoric life in these canyons. The next work to be undertaken should be the excavation and repair of a Mesa Verde pueblo. The extensive mounds of stone and earth on the promontory west of Cliff Palace have not yet been excavated, and offer attractive possibilities for study and a promise of many specimens. Buried in these mounds there are undoubtedly many rooms, secular and ceremonial, which a season's work could uncover, thus enlarging indirectly our knowledge of the cliff-dwellers and their descendants.[2]

The writer considers it an honor to have been placed in charge of the excavation and repair of Cliff Palace, and takes this occasion to express high appreciation of his indebtedness to both the Secretary of the Smithsonian Institution and the Secretary of the Interior for their confidence in his judgment in this difficult undertaking.

Maj. Hans M. Randolph, superintendent of the Mesa Verde National Park, gave assistance in purchasing the equipment, making out accounts, and in other ways. During the sojourn at Cliff Palace the writer was accompanied by Mr. R. G. Fuller, of the Peabody Museum of Harvard University, a volunteer assistant, who contributed some of the photographs used in the preparation of the plates that accompany this report. The writer is indebted also to Mr. F. K. Vreeland, of Montclair, New Jersey, for several fine photographs of Cliff Palace taken before the repairing was done.

---

[2] A few holes that have been dug here and there in these mounds have brought to light sections of walls with good masonry, but no excavations that could be called extensive or scientific have yet been attempted on this site. The excavation of these mounds might reveal a pueblo like Walpi, and a comparison of objects from them with those from Cliff Palace would be important in tracing the relationship of cliff-dwellings and pueblos.

PLATE 2

CLIFF PALACE, FROM THE OPPOSITE SIDE OF THE CANYON.

CLIFF PALACE
A TYPE OF PREHISTORIC CULTURE

In the following pages the walls and other remains of buildings and the objects found in the rooms have been treated from their cultural point of view. Considering ethnology, or culture history, as the comparative study of mental productions of groups of men in different epochs, and cultural archeology as a study of those objects belonging to a time antedating recorded history, there has been sought in Cliff Palace one type of prehistoric American culture, or rather a type of the mental production of a group of men in an environment where, so far as external influences are concerned, caves, mesas, and cliffs are predominant and aridity is a dominant climatic factor. Primarily archeology is a study of the expression of human intelligence, and it must be continually borne in mind that Cliff Palace was once the home of men and women whose minds responded to their surroundings. It is hoped that this monograph will be a contribution to a study of the influence of environment on the material condition of a group of prehistoric people. The condition of culture here brought to light is in part a result of experiences transmitted from one generation to another, but while this heritage of culture is due to environment, intensified by each transmission, there are likewise in it survivals of the culture due to antecedent environments, which have also been preserved by heredity, but has diminished in proportion, pari passu, as the epoch in which they originated is farther and farther removed in time from the environment that created them. These survivals occur mostly in myths and religious cult objects, and are the last to be abandoned when man changes his environment.

It is believed that one advantage of a series of monographic descriptions of these ruins is found in the fact that the characteristics of individual ruins being known, more accurate generalizations concerning the entire culture will later be made possible by comparative studies. There is an individuality in Cliff Palace, not only in its architecture but also in a still greater measure in the symbolism of the pottery decoration. These features vary more or less in different ruins, notwithstanding their former inhabitants were of similar culture. These variations are lost in a general description of that culture.

The reader is asked to bear in mind that when the repair of Cliff Palace was undertaken the vandalism wrought by those who had dug into it had destroyed much data and greatly reduced the possibility of generalizations on the character of its culture. The ruin had been almost completely rifled of its contents, the specimens removed, and its walls left in a very dilapidated condition. Much of the excavation carried on under the writer's supervision yielded meager scientific results so far as the discovery of specimens was concerned; throughout the summer earth was being dug over that had already been examined and cult objects removed. Had it been possible to have begun work on Cliff Palace just after the ruin was deserted by the aboriginal inhabitants, or, as that was impossible, at least anticipated only by the destruction wrought by the elements, these explorations might have illumined many difficult problems which must forever remain unsolved.

The present monograph is the second in a series dealing with the antiquities of the Mesa Verde National Park and opening with the account of the excavation and repair of Spruce-tree House.[3] An exhaustive account of all known antiquities from Cliff Palace is not intended, and no reference is made even to many objects from that ruin now in museums. Discussion of details is not so much aimed at as brevity in the statement of results and a contribution to our knowledge of a typical form of Southwestern culture. Believing that modern Pueblo culture is the direct descendant of that of cliff-dwellers, the writer has not hesitated to make use of ethnology, when possible, in an interpretation of the archeological material.

Although the name Cliff Palace is not altogether an appropriate one for this ruin, it is now too firmly fixed in the literature of cliff-dwellings to be changed. The term "palace" implies a higher social development than that which existed in this village, which undoubtedly had a house chief similar to the village chief (*kimongwi*) of the Hopi, who occupied that position on account of being the oldest man of the oldest clan; but this ruin is not the remains of a "palace" of such a chief.

The population of Cliff Palace was composed of many clans, more or less distinct and independent, which were rapidly being amalgamated by marriage; so we may regard the population as progressing toward a homogeneous community. Cliff Palace was practically a pueblo built in a cave; its population grew from both without and within: new clans from time to time joined those existing, while new births continually augmented the number of inhabitants.

There was no water at Cliff Palace[4] when work began, but a good supply was developed in the canyon below the ruin, where there is every reason to believe the former inhabitants had their well. In a neighboring canyon, separated from that in which Cliff Palace is situated by a promontory at the north, there is also a meager seepage of water which was developed incidentally into a considerable supply. In the cliff above this water is a large cave in which was discovered the walls of a kiva of the second type, but the falling of a large block of rock upon it—which occurred subsequent to the construction of this kiva—led to its abandonment. This cave is extensive enough for a cliff-house as large as Cliff Palace; but for this accident it might have developed into a formidable rival of the latter.

---

[3] *Bulletin 41 of the Bureau of American Ethnology.*

[4] All potable water for camp had to be brought from Spruce-tree House, about 2 miles away.

PLATE 3

THE SOUTHERN END, AFTER AND BEFORE REPAIRING

PHOTOGRAPHED BY R. G. FULLER

RECENT HISTORY

It is remarkable that this magnificent ruin (pl. 1) so long escaped knowledge of white settlers in the neighboring Montezuma valley. Cliff Palace is not mentioned in early Spanish writings, and, indeed, the first description of it was not published until about 1890.

Efforts to learn the name of the white man who discovered Cliff Palace were not rewarded with great success. According to Nordenskiöld it was first seen by Richard Wetherill and Charley Mason on a "December day in 1888," but several residents of the towns of Mancos and Cortez claim to have visited it before that time. One of the first of these visitors was a cattle owner of Mancos, Mr. James Frink, who told the author that he first saw Cliff Palace in 1881, and as several stockmen were with him at that time it is probable that there are others who visited it the same year. We may conclude that Cliff Palace was unknown to scientific men in 1880, and the most we can definitely say is that it was first seen by white men some time in the decade 1880-1890.[5]

While there is considerable literature on the cliff-dwellings of the Mesa Verde, individual ruins have not been exhaustively described. Much less has been published on Spruce-tree House than on Cliff Palace, which latter ruin, being the largest, has attracted more attention than any other in the Park. As every cliff-house has its peculiar architectural features it is well in describing these buildings to refer to the ruins by names. This individuality in architecture pertains likewise to specimens, the majority of which in museums unfortunately are labeled merely "Mancos" or "Mesa Verde." A large number of these objects probably came from Spruce-tree House and Cliff Palace, but it is now impossible to determine their exact derivation.

The first extended account of Cliff Palace, accompanied with illustrations, which is worthy of special mention, was published by Mr. F. H. Chapin, and so far as priority of publication is concerned he may be regarded as the first to make Cliff Palace known to the scientific world. Almost simultaneously with his article there appeared an account of the ruin by Doctor Birdsall, followed shortly by the superbly illustrated memoir of Baron Gustav Nordenskiöld. All these writers adopt the name Cliff Palace, which apparently was first given to the ruin by Richard Wetherill, one of the claimants for its discovery. Nordenskiöld's work contains practically all that was known about Cliff Palace up to the beginning of the summer's field work herein described.

[5] It is generally stated by stockmen and others who claim to have seen Cliff Palace "years ago," that the walls of the buildings were much higher in the early eighties than they are at present.

Mr. Chapin[6] thus referred to Cliff Palace in a paper read before The Appalachian Mountain Club on February 13, 1890:

> After a long ride we reached a camping-ground at the head of a branch of the left-hand fork of Cliff Cañon. Hurriedly unpacking, we hobbled the horses that were the most likely to stray far, and taking along our photographic kit, wended our way on foot toward that remarkable group of ruins of which I have already spoken, and which Richard has called "the Cliff-Palace." At about three o'clock we reached the brink of the cañon opposite the wonderful structure. Surely its discoverer had not overstated the beauty and magnitude of this strange ruin. There it was, occupying a great oval space under a grand cliff wonderful to behold, appearing like an immense ruined castle with dismantled towers. The stones in front were broken away, but behind them rose the walls of a second story; and in the rear of these, in under the dark cavern, stood the third tier of masonry. Still farther back in the gloomy recess, little houses rested on upper ledges. A short distance down the cañon are cosey buildings perched in utterly inaccessible nooks. The neighboring scenery is marvelous; the view down the cañon to the Mancos is alone worth the journey to see. We stopped to take a few views, and then commenced the descent into the gulf below. What would otherwise have been a hazardous proceeding, was rendered easy by using the steps which had been cut in the wall by the builders of the fortress. There are fifteen of these scouped-out hollows in the rock, which covered perhaps half of the distance down the precipice. At that point the cliff had probably fallen away; but luckily for our purpose, a dead tree leaned against the wall, and descending into its branches we reached the base of the parapet. In the bed of the cañon is a secondary gulch, which required care in descending. We hung a rope or lasso over some steep, smooth ledges, and let ourselves down by it. We left it hanging there and used it to ascend by on our return.
>
> Nearer approach increased our interest in the marvel. From the south end of the ruin, which we first attained, trees hide the northern walls, yet the view is beautiful. We remained long, and ransacked the structure from one end to the other. According to Richard's measurements, the space covered by the building is 425 feet long, 80 feet high in front, and 80 feet deep in the centre. One hundred and twenty-four rooms have been traced on the ground floor, and a thousand people may have lived within its confines. So many walls have fallen that it is difficult to reconstruct the building in imagination; but the photographs show that there must have been many stories. There are towers and circular

---

[6] *Appalachia*, vi, 28-30, May, 1890, Boston, 1892.

rooms, square and rectangular enclosures; yet all with a seeming symmetry, though in some places the walls look as if they were put up as additions in later periods. One of the towers is barrel-shaped; other circles are true. The diameter of one circular room, or estufa, is sixteen feet and six inches. There are six piers, which are well plastered. There are five recess-holes, which appear as if constructed for shelves. In several rooms we observed good fireplaces. In another room, where the outer walls have fallen away, we found that an attempt had been made at ornamentation: a broad band had been painted across the wall, and above it is a peculiar decoration which shows in one of our photographs. The lines are similar to embellishment on pottery which we found. We observed in one place corn-cobs imbedded in the plaster in the walls, showing that the cob is as old as that portion of the dwelling. The cobs, as well as kernels of corn which we found, are of small size, similar to what the Ute squaws raise now without irrigation. We found a large stone mortar, which may have been used to grind the corn. Broken pottery was everywhere; like specimens in the other cliff houses, it was similar in design to that which we picked up in the valley ruins near Wetherill's ranch, convincing us of the identity of the builders of the two classes of ruins. We also found parts of skulls and bones, fragments of weapons, and pieces of cloth. One nearly complete skeleton lies on a wall waiting for some future antiquarian. The burial-place of the clan was down under the rear of the cave.

Dr. W. R. Birdsall,[7] who in 1891 gave an account of the cliff-dwellings of the canyons of the Mesa Verde, which contains considerable information regarding these buildings, thus refers specially to Cliff Palace:

Richard Wetherill discovered an unusually large group of buildings which he named "The Cliff Palace," in which the ground plan showed more than one hundred compartments, covering an area over four hundred feet in length and eighty feet in depth in the wider portion. Usually the buildings are continuous where the configuration of the cliffs permitted such construction.

---

[7] *Jour. Amer. Geog. Soc.*, xxiii, no. 4, 598, New York, 1891.

PLATE 4

CENTRAL PART, BEFORE REPAIRING

PHOTOGRAPHED BY F. K. VREELAND

In the following account Baron Nordenskiöld has given us the most exhaustive description of Cliff Palace yet published:[8]

In a long, but not very deep branch of Cliff Cañon, a wild and gloomy gorge named Cliff Palace Cañon, lies the largest of the ruins on the Mesa Verde, the Cliff Palace. Strange and indescribable is the impression on the traveller, when, after a long and tiring ride through the boundless, monotonous piñon forest, he suddenly halts on the brink of the precipice, and in the opposite cliff beholds the ruins of the Cliff Palace, framed in the massive vault of rock above and in a bed of sunlit cedar and piñon trees below (Pl. XII). This ruin well deserves its name, for with its round towers and high walls rising out of the heaps of stones deep in the mysterious twilight of the cavern, and defying in their sheltered site the ravages of time, it resembles at a distance an enchanted castle. It is not surprising that the Cliff Palace so long remained undiscovered. An attempt to follow Cliff Palace Cañon upward from Cliff Cañon meets with almost insurmountable obstacles in the shape of huge blocks of stone which have fallen from the cliffs and formed a barrier across the narrow water course, in most parts of the cañon the only practicable path between the steep walls of rock. Through the piñon forest, which renders the mesa a perfect labyrinth to the uninitiated, chance alone can guide the explorer to the exact spot from which a view of Cliff Palace is possible.

The descent to the ruin may be made from the mesa either on the opposite side of the cañon, or on the same a few hundred paces north or south of the cliff-dwelling. The Cliff Palace is probably the largest ruin of its kind known in the United States. I here give a plan of the ruin (Pl. XI) together with a photograph thereof, taken from the south end of the cave (Pl. XII). In the plan, which represents the ground floor, over a hundred rooms are shown. About twenty of them are estufas. Among the rubbish and stones in front of the ruin a few more walls, not marked in the plan, may possibly be distinguished.

Plate XIII, as I have just mentioned, is a photograph of the Cliff Palace from the south. To the extreme left of the plate a number of much dilapidated walls may be seen. They correspond to rooms 1-12 in the plan. To the right of these walls lies a whole block of rooms (13-18), several stories high and built on a huge rock which has fallen from the roof of the cave. The outermost room (14 in the plan; to the left in Pl. XIII) is bounded on the outside by a high wall, the outlines of which stand off sharply from the dark

[8] In The Cliff Dwellers of the Mesa Verde (a translation in English from the Swedish edition, Stockholm, 1893), (pp. 59-66), unfortunately not accessible to most readers on account of the limited edition and the cost. For this reason the description is here reproduced in extenso. (The references to illustrations and the footnotes in this excerpt follow Nordenskiöld.)

background of the cave. The wall is built in a quadrant at the edge of the rock just mentioned, which has been carefully dressed, the wall thus forming apparently an immediate continuation of the rock. The latter is coursed by a fissure which also extends through the wall. This crevice must therefore have appeared subsequent to the building operation. To the right of this curved wall (still in Pl. XIII) lie four rooms (15-18 in the plan), and in front of them two terraces (21-22) connected by a step. One of the rooms is surrounded by walls three stories high and reaching up to the roof of the cave. The terraces are bounded to the north (the left in Pl. XIII) by a rather high wall, standing apart from the remainder of the building. Not far from the rooms just mentioned, but a little farther back, lie two cylindrical chambers (21 *a*, 23). The wall of 21 *a* is shown in Pl. XIII with a beam resting against it. The beam had been placed there by one of the Wetherills to assist him in climbing to an upper ledge, where low walls, resembling the fortress at Long House (p. 28), rise almost to the roof of the cave. The round room 23 is joined by a wall to a long series of chambers (26-41), which are very low, though their walls extend to the rock above them. They probably served as storerooms. These chambers front on a "street," on the opposite side of which lie a number of apartments[9] (42-50), among them a remarkable estufa (44) described at greater length below. In front of 44 lies another estufa (51), and not far from the latter a third (52).

The "street" leads to an open space. Here lie three estufas (54, 55, 56), partly sunk in the ground. Much lower down is situated another estufa (57) of the same type as 44. It is surrounded by high walls.[10] South of the open space lie a few large rooms (58-61). A tower (63 in the plan; the large tower to the right in Pl. XIII) is situated still farther south, beside a steep ledge. This ledge, north of the tower (to the left in the plate), once formed a free terrace (62), bounded on the outside by a low wall along the margin. South of the tower is an estufa (76) surrounded by an open space, southeast of which are a number of rooms (80-87). In most of them, even in the outermost ones, the walls are in an excellent state of preservation. The wall nearest to the talus slope is 6 metres high and built with great care and skill.[11] South of these rooms and close to the cliff lies a well-preserved estufa (88), and south of the latter four rooms are situated, two of them (90, 92) very small.

[9] The room marked 48 in the plan is visible in Pl. XIII. Almost in the center of the plate, but a little to the right, two small loopholes may be seen, and to their right a doorway, all of which belong to room 48; the walls of 49 and 50 are much lower than those of 48. Behind 48 the high walls of 43 may be distinguished.

[10] They are shown in the plate just to the left of the fold at its middle, rather low down.

[11] A part of this wall may be seen to the extreme right of Pl. XIII, and also in Fig. 34 behind and to the right of the tower.

The walls of the third (91) are very high and rise to the roof of the cave. At one corner the walls have fallen in. This room is figured in a subsequent chapter in order to show a painting found on one of its walls. Near the cliff lies the last estufa (93), in an excellent state of preservation. The rooms south of this estufa are bounded on the outer side by a high wall rising to the rock above it. An excellent defense was thus provided against attack in this quarter.

Two of the estufas in the Cliff Palace deviate from the normal type. This is the only instance where I have observed estufas differing in construction from the ordinary form described in Chapter III. The northern estufa (44 in the plan) is the better preserved of the two. To a height of 1 meter from the floor it is square in form (3×3 m.) with rounded corners (see figs. 35 and 36). Above it is wider and bounded by the walls of the surrounding rooms, a ledge (*b, b*) of irregular shape being thus formed a few feet from the floor. In two of the rounded corners on a level with this ledge (a little to the right in fig. 36) niches or hollows (*d, d*; breadth 48 cm., depth 45 cm.) have been constructed, and between them, at the middle of the south-east wall, a narrow passage (breadth 40 cm.), open at the top. At the bottom of one side of this passage a continuation thereof was found, corresponding probably to the tunnel in estufas of the ordinary type. At the north corner of the room the wall is broken by three small niches (*e, e, e*) quite close together, each of them occupying a space about equal to that left by the removal of two stones from the wall. The sandstone blocks of which the walls are built are carefully hewn, as in the ordinary cylindrical estufas. Whether the usual hearth, in form of a basin, and the wall beside it, had been constructed here I was unfortunately unable to determine, more than half of the room being filled with rubbish. I give the name of estufas to these square rooms with rounded corners, built as described above, because they are furnished with the passage characteristic of the round estufas in the cliff-dwellings. Perhaps they mark the transition to the rectangular estufa of the Moki Indians. Besides the estufas there are some other round rooms or towers (21 *a*, 23, 63), which evidently belonged to the fortifications of the village. They differ from the estufas in the absence of the characteristic passage and also of the six niches. Furthermore, they often contain several stories, and in every respect but the form resemble the rectangular rooms. The long wall just mentioned, built on a narrow ledge above the other ruins, and visible at the top of Pl. XIII was probably another part of the village fortifications. The ledge is situated so near the roof of the cave that the wall, though quite low, touches the latter, and the only way of advancing behind it is to creep on hands and knees.

PLATE 5

THE ROUND TOWER, FROM THE NORTH GENERAL VIEW OF THE RUIN,
BEFORE REPAIRING

GENERAL VIEW OF THE RUIN, BEFORE REPAIRING

PHOTOGRAPHED BY F. K. VREELAND

A comparison between Pl. VIII and Pl. XIII shows at once that the inhabitants of the Cliff Palace were further advanced in architecture than their more western kinsfolk on the Mesa Verde. The stones are carefully dressed and often laid in regular courses; the walls are perpendicular, sometimes leaning slightly inwards at the same angle all round the room — this being part of the design. All the corners form almost perfect right angles, when the surroundings have permitted the builders to observe this rule. This remark also applies to the doorways, the sides of which are true and even. The lintel often consists of a large stone slab, extending right across the opening. On closer observation we find that in the Cliff Palace we may discriminate two slightly different methods of building. The lower walls, where the stones are only rough-hewn and laid without order, are often surmounted by walls of carefully dressed blocks in regular courses. This circumstance suggests that the cave was inhabited during two different periods. I shall have occasion below to return to this question.

The rooms of the Cliff Palace seem to have been better provided with light and air than the cliff-dwellings in general, small peep-holes appearing at several places in the walls. The doorways, as in other cliff-dwellings, are either rectangular or T-shaped. Some of the latter are of unusual size, in one instance 1.05 m. high and 0.81 m. broad at the top. The thickness of the walls is generally about 0.3 m., sometimes, in the outer walls, as much as 0.6 m. As a rule they are not painted, but in some rooms covered with a thin coat of yellow plaster. At the south end of the ruin lies an estufa (93) which is well-preserved (fig. 37). This estufa is entered by a doorway in the wall, one of the few instances where I have observed this arrangement. In most cases, as I have already mentioned, the entrance was probably constructed in the roof. The dimensions of this estufa were as follows: diameter 3.9 m., distance from the floor to the bottom of the niches 1.2 m., height of the niches 0.9 m., breadth of the same 1.3 m., depth of the same 0.5 to 1.3 m., height of the passage at its mouth 0.75 m., breadth of the same 0.45 m. Five small quadrangular holes or niches were scattered here and there in the lower part of the wall.

I cannot refrain from once more laying stress on the skill to which the walls of Cliff Palace in general bear witness, and the stability and strength which has been supplied to them by the careful dressing of the blocks and the chinking of the interstices with small chips of stone. A point remarked by Jackson in his description of the ruins of Southwestern Colorado, is that the finger marks of the mason may still be traced in the mortar, and that those marks are so small as to suggest that the work of building was performed by women. This conclusion seems too hasty, for within the range of my observations the size of the finger marks varies not a little.

Like Sprucetree House and other large ruins the Cliff Palace contains at the back of the cave extensive open spaces where tame turkeys were probably kept. In this part of the village three small rooms, isolated from the rest of the building, occupy a position close to the cliff; two of them (103, 104), built of large flat slabs of stones, lie close together, the third (105), of unhewn sandstone (fig. 38), is situated farther north. These rooms may serve as examples of the most primitive form of architecture among the cliff people.

In the Cliff Palace, the rooms lie on different levels, the ground occupied by them being very rough. In several places terraces have been constructed in order to procure a level foundation, and here as in their other architectural labours, the cliff-dwellers have displayed considerable skill.

One very remarkable circumstance in the Cliff Palace is that all the pieces of timber, all the large rafters, have disappeared. The holes where they passed into the walls may still be seen, but throughout the great block of ruins two or three large beams are all that remain. This is the reason why none of the rooms is completely closed. At Sprucetree House there were a number of rooms where the placing of the door stone in position was enough to throw the room into perfect darkness, no little aid to the execution of photographic work. It is difficult to explain the above state of things. I observed the same want of timber in parts of other ruins (at Long House for example). In several of the cliff-dwellings it appears as if the beams had purposely been removed from the walls to be applied to some other use. Seldom, however, have all the rafters disappeared, as in the Cliff Palace. There are no traces of the ravages of fire. Perhaps the inhabitants were forced, during the course of a siege, to use the timber as fuel; but in that case it is difficult to understand how a proportionate supply of provisions and water was obtained. This is one of the numerous circumstances which are probably connected with the extinction or migration of the former inhabitants, but from which our still scanty information of the cliff-dwellers cannot lift the veil of obscurity.

PLATE 6

CENTRAL PART, AFTER REPAIRING

PHOTOGRAPHED BY R. G. FULLER

In addition to his description Nordenskiöld gives a ground plan of Cliff Palace[12] (pl. xi); a magnificent double page view of the ruin from the west (pl. xiii); a fine picture of Speaker-chief's House (pl. xii); a view of the Round Tower (fig. 34); a figure and a plan of an estufa of singular construction (T); a view of the interior of Kiva C and of a small room at the back of the main rows of rooms. No specimens of pottery, stone implements, and kindred antiquities from Cliff Palace are figured by Nordenskiöld. In various places throughout his work this author refers to Cliff Palace in a comparative way, and in his descriptions of other ruins the student will find more or less pertaining to it.

In his book The Cliff Dwellers and Pueblos,[13] Rev. Stephen D. Peet devotes one chapter (VII) to Cliff Palace and its surroundings, compiling and quoting from Chapin, Birdsall, and Nordenskiöld. No new data appear in this work, and the illustrations are copied from these authors.

Dr. Edgar L. Hewett[14] briefly refers to Cliff Palace as follows (p. 54):

> Il suffira de décrire les traits principaux d'un seul groupement de ruines, et nous choisirons Cliff Palace, qui en est le spécimen le plus remarquable (pl. I *b*). Il est situé dans un bras de Ruin Canyon. La vue présentée ici est prise d'un point plus élevé, au sud, d'où l'on contemple les ruines d'une ville ancienne, avec des tours rondes et carrées, des maisons, des entrepôts pour le grain, des habitations et des lieux de culte. Le Cliff Palace remplit une immense caverne bien défendue et à l'abri des ravages des éléments. Un sentier conduit aux ruines. Le plan (Fig. 2) représente les restes de 105 chambres au plain-pied. On ne sait combien il y en avait dans les 3 étages supérieurs, mais il est probable que Cliff-Palace n'abritait pas moins de 500 personnes.
>
> Nous remarquons à Cliff-Palace de grands progrès dans l'art de la construction. Les murs sont faits de grès gris, taillé avec des outils de pierre, dont on voit encore les traces. Lorsqu'on se servait de pierres irrégulières, les crevasses étaient remplies avec des fragments ou des éclats de grès, puis on plâtrait les murs avec du mortier d'adobe. On prenait de grosses poutres pour les plafonds et les planchers, et l'on peut voir que ces poutres étaient dégrossies avec des instruments peu tranchants.

Many newspaper and magazine accounts of the Mesa Verde ruins appeared about the time Mr. Chapin's description was published, but the majority of these are somewhat distorted and more or less exaggerated, often too indefinite for scientific purposes. References to them, even if here quoted, could hardly be of great

---

[12] The illustrations referred to in this paragraph are in Nordenskiöld's work.

[13] As stated in a note (Peet, p. 133) Chapter VII is a reprint of Doctor Birdsall's article in the *Journal of the American Geographical Society*, op. cit.

[14] In Les Communautés Anciennes dans le Désert Américain. In this work may be found a ground plan of Cliff Palace by Morley and Kidder, the interior of kiva Q (pl. viii, *e*), and a large view of the ruin taken from the north (pl. i, *b*). (Plate and figure designations from Hewett.)

value to the reader, as in most cases it would be impossible for him to consult files of papers in which they occur even if the search were worth while. Much that they record is practically a compilation from previous descriptions.

The activity in photographing Cliff Palace has done much to make known its existence and structure. Many excellent photographs of the ruin have been taken, among which may be mentioned those of Chapin, Nordenskiöld, Vreeland, Nusbaum, and others. Oil paintings, some of which are copied from photographs, others made from the ruin itself, adorn the walls of some of our museums. Almost every visitor to the Mesa Verde carries with him a camera, and many good postal cards with views of the ruin are on the market. Negatives of Cliff Palace taken before its excavation and repair will become more valuable as time passes, because they can no longer be duplicated. From a study of a considerable number of these photographs it seems that very little change has taken place in the condition of the ruin between the time the first pictures were made and the repair work was begun.

SITE OF CLIFF PALACE

Cliff Palace is situated in a cave in Cliff-palace canyon, a branch of Cliff canyon, which is here about 200 feet deep. It occupies practically the whole of the cave, the roof of which overhangs about two-thirds of the ruin, projecting considerably beyond its middle. This cave is much more capacious than that in which Spruce-tree House is situated, as shown by comparing illustrations and descriptions of the latter in the former report. The configuration of Spruce-tree House cave and that of Cliff Palace, and the relation of its floor to the talus, also differ. The canyon in which Cliff Palace lies is thickly wooded, having many cedars and a few pines and scrub oaks; the almost total failure of water at certain seasons of the year at Cliff Palace renders floral life in the vicinity less exuberant than in Spruce-tree canyon, a branch of Navaho canyon (fig. 1). On the level plateau above the ruin there are many trees—pines and cedars—but even this area is not so thickly wooded as the summit of the mesa above Spruce-tree House.[15]

The geological formation of the cave in which Cliff Palace is situated is similar to that at Spruce-tree House, consisting of alternating layers of hard and soft sandstone, shale, and even layers of coal. Both canyons and caves appear to have been formed by the same processes. In past ages the elements have eroded and undermined the soft layers of sandstone or shale to such an extent that great blocks of rock, being left without foundations, have broken away from above, falling down the precipice. Many of these great bowlders remained on the floor of a cave where it was broad enough to retain them. The surface of the roof arching over Cliff Palace cave is perhaps smoother than that of Spruce-tree House. The progress of cave erosion was greatly augmented by the flow of water from the mesa summit during heavy rains, as hereinafter described.

---

[15] Clearings in the forest indicate the positions of the former farms of the inhabitants of Cliff Palace.

PLATE 7

SOUTHERN END, AFTER REPAIRING

PHOTOGRAPHED BY R. G. FULLER

FIG. 1.—VIEW DOWN NAVAHO CANYON.

To understand the general plan of Cliff Palace it is necessary to take into consideration the method of formation and the configuration of the cave floor on which the ruin stands. This cave, as already stated, was formed by erosion or undercutting the softer rock at a lower level than the massive sandstone, leaving huge blocks of stone above the eroded cavities. Naturally these blocks, being without support, fell, and in falling were broken, the larger fragments remaining on the floor practically in the places where they fell, but many of the smaller stones were washed out of the cave entrance, forming a talus extending down the side of the cliff. The floor of the cave was thus strewn with stones, large and small, resting on the same general level which is that on which the foundations of the buildings were constructed. The level of the cave floor was interrupted by the huge blocks of stone forming its outer margin; and the buildings constructed on these fallen rocks were lofty, even imposing. The talus composed of fallen rock and débris, piled against the canyon side in front of these buildings and below these huge blocks of stone, extends many feet down the cliff in a gradual slope, covering the terraced buildings and burying their retaining walls from sight.[16] A great part of this talus is composed of fallen walls, but considerable earth and small stones are contained in it, probably precipitated over the rim of the cave roof by the torrents of water which sometimes fall during heavy rains. It is probable also that the foresting of the talus has been due more or less to bushes and small trees washed over the cliff from the mesa summit.

Three terraces or tiers containing rooms, as shown in the accompanying ground plan, were revealed by excavations in this talus. At the western extension, where the second and third terraces cease, the tops of large rocks begin at the level of the fourth terrace, and on the southern end the first terrace is absent. At the western extremity, the large blocks of rock having dropped down entire from the side of the cliff, fill the interval elsewhere occupied by the lower terraces, and their tops now form a ledge upon which rest the foundations of rooms level with the plaza. It is thus evident that whereas the front wall of Spruce-tree House is simple, the level of the kiva roofs and floors of buildings above ground being continuous, the front of Cliff Palace is complicated, being at different levels, consisting of terraces in the talus. As one approached Cliff Palace, when inhabited, it must have presented, from below, an imposing structure, the lower terraces being occupied by many large kivas above which rose lofty buildings arranged in tiers, several being four stories high. Although the height was much increased by the presence of huge foundation blocks of sandstone, from the lowest terrace to the highest room there were seven floor levels, including those of the kivas in the terraces.

An examination of Cliff Palace cave shows that from the southern end to the section over the main entrance its roof arches upward and that the part over the rear of the ruin is lower than that over its front. Between the lower and upper roof levels there is a sharp break formed by a vertical cleavage plane. Where this plane joins the upper level there is a shelf forming a recess in which has been constructed a row of ledge rooms.[17]

The great rock roof arching over Cliff Palace is broken about midway between the vertical plane above mentioned and the rim by another and narrower vertical plane where no ledge exists. Here multitudes of swallows had made their home, and there are wasps' nests in several places.

---

[16] Access to Cliff Palace from the bottom of the canyon, although difficult, is possible, and a pathway might be constructed down its sides or along the top of the talus to several other cliff-dwellings. In the vicinity of Cliff Palace there are at least 20 ruins, large and small.

[17] One of these rooms had been chosen by eagles for their nests, but both nests and eggs were abandoned by the birds after the repair work was begun.

PLATE 8

GROUND PLAN

FROM SURVEY BY R. G. FULLER

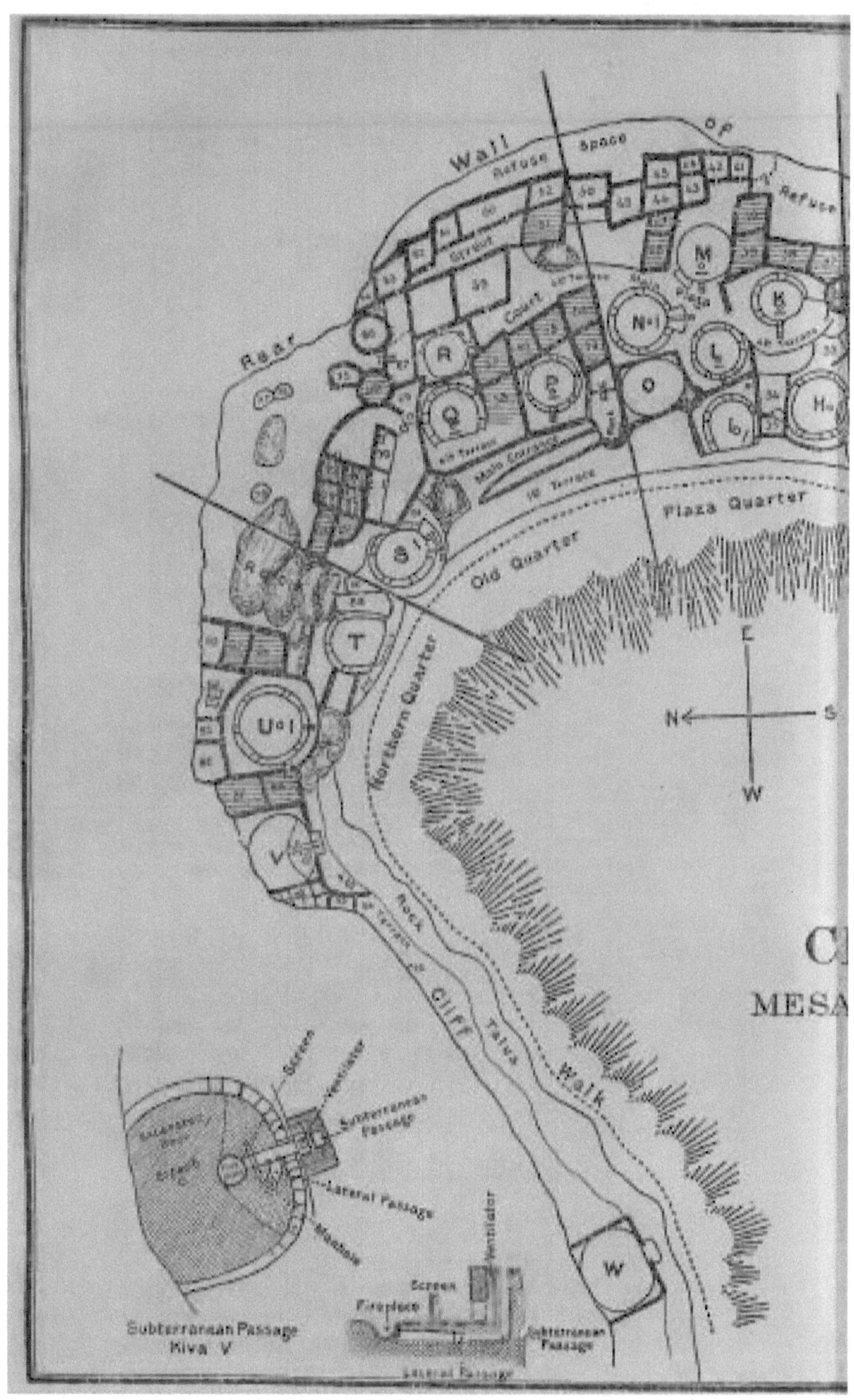

(Enlarged - Left)

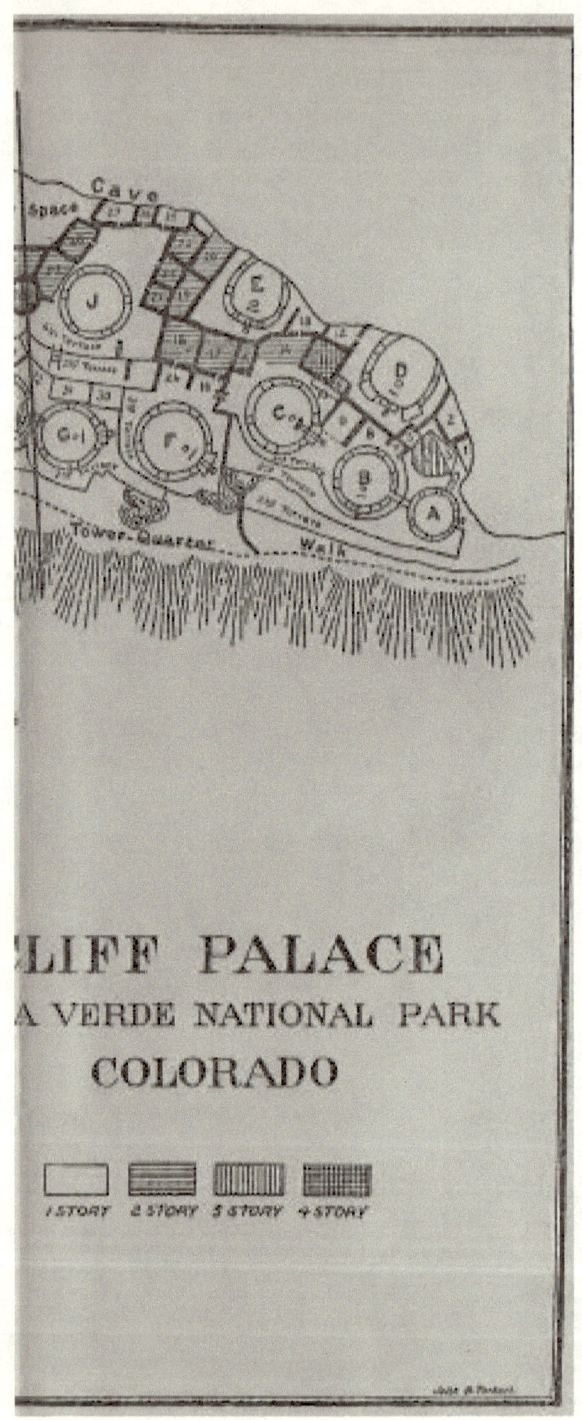

(Enlarged - Right)

PREHISTORIC TRAILS TO CLIFF PALACE

It is evident that the prehistoric farmers of Cliff Palace repeatedly visited their fields among the cedars on top of the mesa, and well-worn trails led from their habitation to these clearings. Several such trails have long been known, one of which was formerly exclusively used by white visitors and was facetiously called "Fat Man's Misery." To another ancient pathway, near which ladders were placed, the name "Ladder Trail" may be applied. The pathways now used by visitors follow approximately these old trails, which were simply series of shallow footholes cut in the cliff. Although the lapse of time since they were pecked in the rock has somewhat diminished their depth, they can still be used by an adventurous climber.

GENERAL FEATURES

Cliff Palace (pls. 1, 2), the most instructive cliff-house yet discovered in the Mesa Verde National Park, if not in the United States, is one of the most picturesque ruins in the Southwest. While its general contour follows that of the rear of the cave in which it is situated, its two extremities project beyond the cavern. The entire central part is protected by the cave roof; the ends are exposed.

The general orientation of Cliff Palace is north and south, the cave lying at the eastern end of the canyon of which it is an extension. The southern end is practically outside this cave, and the few rooms westward from kiva V are unprotected. An isolated kiva, W, with high surrounding walls, is situated some distance beyond the extreme western end of the ruin. Although not in the same cave as the main ruin, certain other rooms in the vicinity of Cliff Palace may have been ceremonially connected with it. They are built in shallow depressions in the cliffs and may have been shrines or rooms to which priests retreated for the purpose of performing their rites. In the category of dependent structures may also be mentioned numerous rings of stones on top of the mesa. The existence of calcined human bones in the soil over which these stones are heaped indicates the practice of cremation, of which there is also evidence in the ruin itself.

DESTRUCTION BY THE ELEMENTS

The constant beating of rain and snow, often accompanied in winter by freezing of water in the crevices of the masonry, has sadly dilapidated a large part of the front walls of Cliff Palace, especially those at the northern and southern ends (pl. 3) where they do not have the protection of the overhanging roof of the cave.

While the sections known as the old quarter, the plaza quarter, and much of the tower quarter are protected by the roof of the cave, even here there has been exposure and destruction from the same cause. Torrential rains on the mesa in the late summer form streams of water which, following depressions,[18] flow over the rim of the cave roof and are precipitated into the trees beyond the lowest terrace of the ruin. The destruction of walls from these flows is much less than that from smaller streams which, following the edge of the cave roof, run under the roof and drip on the walls, washing the mortar from between the component stones, and eventually undermining their foundation and leading to their fall. The former presence of these streams is indicated by the black discoloration of the cave roof

---

[18] In some of these waterways are found good examples of "potholes," some of considerable size, which often retain water for a long time. Their capacity was increased in prehistoric times by the construction of dams.

shown in photographs.

A visitor to Cliff Palace in the dry season can hardly imagine the amount of rain that occasionally falls during the summer months, and it is difficult for him to appreciate the destructive force it exerts when precipitated over the cliff. When Cliff Palace was occupied, damage to walls could be immediately repaired by the inhabitants after every torrent, but as the ruin remained for centuries uninhabited and without repair, the extent of the destruction was great. The torrents falling over the ruin not only gain force from the distance of the fall, but sweep everything before them, bringing down earth, stones, small trees, and bushes. At such a time the bottom of the canyon is filled with a roaring torrent fed by waterfalls that can be seen at intervals far down the gorge. The observer standing in Cliff Palace during such a downpour can behold a sheet of water falling over the projecting cliff in front of him. These cataracts fortunately are never of long duration, but while they last their power is irresistible.[19]

VANDALISM

No ruin in the Mesa Verde Park had suffered more from the ravages of "pot hunters" than Cliff Palace; indeed it had been much more mutilated than the other ruins in the park (pls. 1, 4, 5). Parties of workmen had remained at the ruin all winter, and many specimens had been taken from it and sold. There was good evidence that the workmen had wrenched beams from the roofs and floors to use for firewood, so that not a single roof and but few rafters remained in place. However, no doubt many of the beams had been removed, possibly by cliff-dwellers, long before white men first visited the place.

Many of the walls had been broken down and their foundations undermined, leaving great rents through them to let in light or to allow passage from the débris thrown in the rooms as dumping places. Hardly a floor had not been dug into, and some of the finest walls had been demolished.[20] All this was done to obtain pottery and other minor antiquities that had a market value. The arrest of this vandalism is fortunate and shows an awakened public sentiment, but it can not repair the irreparable harm that has been done.

---

[19] While there has probably been considerable erosion in the bed of the canyon since Cliff Palace was constructed, this does not mean that "the action of the water carved out the valley, leaving at an inaccessible height buildings originally constructed on almost level land." See History N. Y. State Chapter, Colorado Cliff Dwellings Assoc., p. 11.

[20] Some, possibly considerable, of this mutilation may be ascribed to the former occupants. The Ute Indians will not now enter cliff-dwellings and probably are not responsible for their destruction.

PLATE 9

MAIN ENTRANCE SOUTHERN END, SHOWING REPAIRED TERRACES

SOUTHERN END, SHOWING REPAIRED TERRACES

REPAIR OF WALLS

The masonry work necessary to repair a ruin as large and as much demolished as Cliff Palace was very considerable. The greatest amount was expended on those walls in front of the cave floor hidden under the lower terraces, at the northern and southern extremities. The latter portion was so completely destroyed that it had to be rebuilt in some places, while at the southern end an equal amount of repair work was necessary. (pls. 3, 6, 7, 9.) To permanently protect these sections of the ruin the tops of the walls and the plazas were liberally covered with Portland cement, and runways were constructed to carry off the surface water into gutters by which it was diverted over the retaining walls to fall on the rock foundations beyond. It would be impossible permanently to protect some of these exposed walls without constructing roofs above them; at present every heavy rain is bound to cover the floors of the kivas with water and thus eventually to undermine their foundations.

The preservation of walls deep in the cave under protection of the roof was not a difficult problem. The work in this part consisted chiefly in the repair of kiva walls, building them to their former height at the level of neighboring plazas.

MAJOR ANTIQUITIES

Under this term are embraced those immovable objects as walls of houses and their various structural parts—floors, roofs, and fireplaces. These features must of necessity be protected in place and left where they were constructed. Minor antiquities, as implements of various kinds, stone objects, pottery, textiles, and the like, can best be removed and preserved in a museum, where they can be seen to greater advantage and by a much larger number of people. The ideal way would be to preserve both major and minor antiquities together in the same neighborhood, or to install the latter in the places in which they were found. While at present such an arrangement at Spruce-tree House and Cliff Palace is not practicable, large specimens, as metates and those jars that are embedded in the walls, have, as a rule, been left as they were found.

As the repair work at Cliff Palace was limited to the protection of the major antiquities, the smaller objects for the greater part having been removed before our work began, this report deals more especially with the former, the whole ruin being regarded as a great specimen to be preserved in situ.

Very little attention was given to labeling rooms, kivas, and their different parts, the feeling being that this experiment has been sufficiently well carried out at Spruce-tree House, an examination of which would logically precede that of Cliff Palace. Spruce-tree House has been made a "type ruin" from which the tourist can gain his first impression of the major antiquities of the Mesa Verde National Park, and while it was well to indicate on its walls the different features characteristic of these buildings, it would be redundant to carry out the same plan in the other ruins.[21]

---

[21] The author's hope is to excavate and repair in different sections of the Southwest a number of "type ruins," each of which will illustrate the major antiquities of the area in

No attempt was made to restore the roof of any of the Cliff Palace kivas for the reason that one can gain a good idea of how the roof of a circular kiva is constructed from its restoration in Kiva C of Spruce-tree House, and an effort to roof a kiva of Cliff Palace would merely duplicate what has already been accomplished without adding essentially to our knowledge.

which it occurs. From an examination of these types the tourist and the student may obtain, at first hand, an accurate knowledge of the prehistoric architecture.

GENERAL PLAN OF CLIFF PALACE

The ground plans of Cliff Palace which have been published were made from surface indications before excavations were undertaken and necessarily do not represent all the rooms. Nordenskiöld's map outlines 17 kivas and 102 rooms, indicating several kivas by dotted lines. The Morley-Kidder map, which represents positions of 18 or 19 kivas, notes 105 secular rooms.[22] Although this ground plan is an improvement on that of Nordenskiöld, it also was based on surface indications and naturally fails to indicate those kivas that were buried under the fallen walls of the terraces. Strangely enough, in Nordenskiöld's ground plan Kiva K is omitted, notwithstanding the tops of one or two pilasters were readily seen before any excavation was made. Neither of these plans distinguishes those buildings that have more than a single story, although they show the parts of walls that extend to the roof. Neither Chapin nor Birdsall published maps of Cliff Palace. (See pl. 8.)

TERRACES AND RETAINING WALLS

The terraces in front of the rooms occupying the floor of the cave are characteristic features of Cliff Palace (pls. 9, 10). The excavations revealed three of these terraces, of which the floor of the cave is the fourth. This fourth terrace, or cave floor, is in the main horizontal, but on account of the accumulated talus the slope from the southern end of the portion in front of kiva G was gradual and continued at about this level to the northern end of the ruin. This slope brought it about that kivas in the terraces are at different levels. The floors of kivas H and I lie on about the level of the first terrace, that of G on the terrace above, and F lies on the third terrace; the remaining kivas are all excavated in the cave floor, or fourth terrace. From the main entrance to the ruin, extending northward, there are representations of the second and third terraces, both of which extend to the cliff in front of kiva U. It is probable from the general appearance of the ruin that when all the terraces and walls were intact Cliff Palace was also terraced with houses along the front, which recalls architectural features in certain cliff-dwellings in Canyon de Chelly.

---

[22] In "Report, House of Representatives, No. 3703, 58th Congress," Mr. Coert Dubois ascribes to Cliff House (Cliff Palace) 146 rooms and 5 estufas (kivas). Unfortunately the error in the count of kivas has been given wide circulation. As stated in the present article, there are at least 23 rooms in Cliff Palace that may be called kivas.

PLATE 10

TOWER QUARTER, AFTER REPAIRING

TERRACES AT SOUTHERN END, AFTER REPAIRING

TOWER QUARTER

For convenience of description Cliff Palace is arbitrarily divided into four quarters, known as tower quarter, plaza quarter, old quarter, and northern quarter. The tower quarter (pls. 10-14) occupies the whole southern portion of the ruin and extends to the extreme southern end from a line drawn perpendicular to the cliff through the round tower. It includes 8 kivas, A to G, and J, 6 of which, A, B, C, D, E, and J, are situated on the fourth terrace, the level of the kiva floor being that of the third terrace. Kiva F lies in the third, and G in the second terrace. It will be seen from an inspection of the ground plan that there are in all 29 rooms in this quarter, besides the 8 kivas, an instructive fact when compared with Spruce-tree House with its 8 kivas and 114 rooms. It must be remembered that several of the rooms in this quarter are of two stories, one is of three stories, and one of four stories, thus adding from 15 to 20 rooms to the 8 enumerated as occupying the ground floor. The proportion of ceremonial rooms to kivas in this quarter would be a little more than 2 to 1.

PLAZA QUARTER

The plaza quarter, as its name indicates, is a large open space, the floor of which is formed mainly by the contiguous roofs of the several kivas (K to O) that are sunk below it. The main entrance to the village opens into this plaza at its northwestern corner, and on the northern side it is continued into a court which connects with the main street or alley of the cliff village. From its position, relations, and other considerations, it is supposed that this quarter was an important section of Cliff Palace and that here were held some of the large open-air gatherings of the inhabitants of the place; here also no doubt were celebrated the sacred dances which we have every reason to believe were at times performed by the former inhabitants. The roof levels of kivas H and I did not contribute to the size of the main plaza, but show good evidence of later construction. Judging from the number of fireplaces in this quarter there is reason to believe that much cooking was done in this open space, in addition to its use for ceremonial or other gatherings of the inhabitants.

OLD QUARTER

The section of Cliff Palace that has been designated the old quarter (pls. 14, 15) lies between a line drawn from the main entrance of the ruin to the rear of the cave and the extreme northern end, culminating in a high castle-like cluster of rooms. It may well be called one of the most important sections of Cliff Palace, containing, as it does, the largest number of rooms, the most varied architecture, and the best masonry. Its protected situation under the roof of the cave is such that we may consider it and the adjoining plaza quarter the earliest settled sections of the village. It contains all varieties of inclosures known in cliff-dwellings: kivas of two types, round rooms, rectangular rooms, an alley or a street, and a court. The floor of the cave on which the rooms are built is broadest at this point, which is one of the best protected sites and the least accessible to enemies in the whole building. It may be theoretically supposed that originally the kiva quarter was an annex of this section and that some of the kivas in this quarter may also have been owned and used by the clans which founded Cliff Palace. The old quarter is divided into two parts, a northern and a southern, the former being arbitrarily designated the Speaker-chief's House. The "street" running approximately north and south bisects the old quarter, making a front and a rear section.

NORTHERN QUARTER

This quarter (pl. 16) of Cliff Palace extends from the high rocks on which the Speaker-chief's House is perched, in a westerly direction, ending with a milling room and adjacent inclosures 92 to 94, situated west of kiva V. It includes three kivas; two, U and V, being situated on the fourth terrace; and one, T, on the first terrace. Kivas U and V are built on top of large rocks, the floor of kiva V being excavated in solid rock. Much of this quarter, especially the western end, is under the sky, and consequently without the protection of the cave roof, on which account it was considerably destroyed by rain water flowing over the canyon rim. The walls of this quarter, especially where it joins the old quarter, exhibit fine masonry, suggesting that it was inhabited by important clans.

MASONRY

The walls of Cliff Palace present the finest masonry known to any cliff-dwelling and among the best stonework in prehistoric ruins north of Mexico. A majority of the stones used in the construction were well dressed before laying and smoothed after they were set in the wall. The joints are often broken, but it is rare to find intersecting walls or corners bonded. Stones of approximately the same size are employed, thereby making the courses, as a rule, level. Although commonly the foundations are composed of the largest stones, this is not an invariable rule, often larger stones being laid above smaller ones; the latter, even when used for foundations, are sometimes set on edge. As a rule, the walls are not plumb or straight. The custom of laying stone foundations on wooden beams is shown in several instances, especially in cases where it was necessary to bridge the intervals between projecting rocks. The arch was unknown to the masons of Cliff Palace; there are no pillars to support floors or roofs as in Spruce-tree House. It is not rare, especially in the kivas, to find instances of double or reenforced walls which may or may not be bonded by connecting stones.

The masonry of the kivas as a rule is superior to that of the secular rooms. The mortar employed in the construction is hard; the joints are chinked with spalls, fragments of pottery, or clay balls. The fact that much more mortar than was necessary was employed resulted in weakening the walls. Several walls were laid without mortar; in some of these the joints were pointed, in others not.[23] The ancient builders did not always seek solid bases for foundations, but built their walls in several instances on ashes or sand, evidently not knowing when the foundations were laid that other stories would later be constructed upon them.

------

[23] Fragments of mortar from the walls and floors, ground to powder, were used in the repair work.

PLATE 11

TOWER QUARTER

PHOTOGRAPHED BY R. G. FULLER

In several sections of the ruin there are evidences that old walls, apparently of houses formerly used, served in part as walls for new buildings. There are also several instances of secondary construction in which old entrances are walled up or even buried and old passageways covered with new structures. Similar reconstruction is common in Hopi pueblos, where it has led to enlargement of rooms and other variations in form. Among the several examples of such secondary building in Cliff Palace may be mentioned a long wall, evidently the front of a large building, which serves as a rear wall of several rooms arranged side by side. The obvious explanation of such a condition is that the walls of the small rooms are of later construction.

As above mentioned the foundations of many walls are of larger stones, and the masonry here is coarser than higher up, which has led some authors to ascribe this fact as due to two epochs of construction. But this conclusion does not appear to be wholly justifiable, although there is evidence in many places that there has been rebuilding over old walls and consequent modification in new constructions, by which older walls have ceased to be necessary, a condition not unlike that existing in several of the Hopi pueblos. In this category may be included the several doors and windows that have been filled in with new masonry or even concealed by new walls. From the fragile character of certain foundations of high walls it would appear that it was not the intention, when they were laid, to erect on them walls more than one story high; the construction of higher stories upon them was an afterthought. Evidences occur of repair of breaks in the walls and corners by the aboriginal occupants, one of the most apparent of which appears at the end of the court in the southern wall of room 59.

ADOBE BRICKS

The walls, as a rule, were made of stone; indeed it is unusual to find adobe walls in cliff-dwellings of the Mesa Verde. In prehistoric buildings in our Southwest, evidences that the ancients made adobe bricks, sun-dried before laying, are very rare. Bricks made of clay are set in the walls of the Speaker-chief's House and were found in the fallen débris at its base. These bricks were made cubical in form before laying, but there is nothing to prove that they were molded in forms or frames, nor do they have a core of straw as in the case of the adobes used in the construction of Inscription House in the Navaho National Monument, Arizona.[24] The use of adobes in the construction of cliff-house walls has not been previously mentioned, although we find references to "lumps of clay" in the earliest historic times among Pueblos. Thus the inhabitants of Tiguex, according to Castañeda, were acquainted with adobes. "They collect," says this author, "great heaps of thyme and rushes and set them on fire; when the mass is reduced to ashes and charcoal they cast a great quantity of earth and water upon it and mix the whole together. They knead this stuff into round lumps, which they learn to dry and use instead of stone."

---

[24] See *Bulletin 50, Bureau of American Ethnology.*

PLATE 12

THE SQUARE TOWER, BEFORE AND AFTER REPAIRING

PHOTOGRAPHED BY R. G. FULLER

Attention may be called to the fact that not only the adobes found at Cliff Palace but also the mortar used in the construction of the walls contain ashes and sometimes even small fragments of charcoal. Clay or adobe plastered on osiers woven between upright sticks, so common in the walls of cliff-dwellings in Canyon de Chelly and in the ruins in the Navaho Monument, while not unknown in the Mesa Verde, is an exceptional method of construction and was not observed at Cliff Palace. The survival[25] of this method of building a wall, if survival it be, may be seen in the deflector of kiva K.

PLASTERING

The walls of a number of rooms were coated with a layer of plastering of sand or clay. This was found on the outside of some walls, where it is generally worn, but it is best preserved on the interior surfaces. Perhaps the most striking examples of plastering on exterior walls occurs on the Speaker-chief's House, where the smoothness of the finish is noteworthy.

From impressions of hands and fingers on this plastering it is evident that it was laid on not with trowels but with the hands, and as the impressions of hands are small the plasterers were probably women or children. In several instances where the plastering is broken several successive layers are seen, often in different colors, sometimes separated by a thin black layer deposited by smoke. The color of the plastering varies considerably, sometimes showing red, often yellow or white, depending on the different colored sand or mud employed.[26] The plastering not only varies in color but also in thickness and in finish. In the most protected rooms of the cave practically all the superficial plastering still remains on both the interior and the exterior of the walls, but for the greater part it has been washed from the surfaces and out of the joints in the outer buildings. The mortar was evidently rubbed smooth with the hands, aided, perhaps, with flat stones. The exterior of one or two rooms shows several coats of plaster, and different parts of the same walls are of different colors. Indistinct figures are scratched on several walls, but the majority of these are too obscure to be traced or deciphered. The plastering on the exterior and the interior of the same wall is often of different color.

PAINTINGS AND ROCK MARKINGS

Figures are painted on the white plastering of the third story of room 11 and on the lower border of the banquette of kiva I, the former being the most elaborate mural paintings known in cliff-dwellings, showing several symbols which are reproduced on pottery. A reversed symbolic rain-cloud figure, painted white,

---

[25] In at least one of the Oraibi kivas the plastering of the wall is laid on sticks that form a kind of lathing. Whether this is a survival of an older method of construction or is traceable to European influence has not been determined, but it is believed to be a survival of prehistoric wall construction.

[26] The red color is derived from the red soil common everywhere on the mesa. Yellow was obtained from disintegrated rock, and white is a marl which is found at various places. The mortar used by the ancient masons became harder, almost cement, when made of marl mixed with adobe.

occurs on the exterior of the low ledge house.[27] Mural paintings of unusual form are found on the under side of the projecting rock forming part of the floor of room 3, and there are scratches on the plastering of the wall of kiva K. The latter figures were intended to represent animals, heads of grotesque beings, possibly birds, and terraced designs symbolic of rain clouds. As one or more of these symbols occur on pottery fragments, there appears no doubt that both were made by the same people. Among rock markings may also be mentioned shallow, concave grooves made by rubbing harder stones, which can be seen on the cliffs in front of rooms 92 and 93 and in the court west of room 51.

Among the figures painted on whitewashed walls of room 11 may be mentioned triangles, parallel red lines with dots, and a square figure, in red, crossed by zigzags, recalling the designs on old Navaho blankets.

The parallel lines are placed vertically and are not unlike, save in color, those which the Hopi make with prayer meal on the walls of their kivas, in certain ceremonies. But it is to be noted that the Hopi markings are made horizontally instead of vertically, as at Cliff Palace. The dots represented on the sides of some of these parallel lines (room 11) are similar to those appearing on straight lines or triangles in the decoration of Mesa Verde pottery. The triangular figures still used by the Hopi in decorating the margins of dados in their houses also occur on some of the Cliff-Palace walls, but are placed in a reversed position. They are said to represent a butterfly, a rain cloud, or a sex symbol. It is interesting to note in passing that two or more triangles placed one above another appear constantly in the same position in Moorish tile and stucco decorations, but this, of course, is only a coincidence, as there is no evidence of a cultural connection.

---

[27] This figure resembles closely that on the outside walls of the third story of room 11 of Spruce-tree House. (See pls. 4, 5, 6, *Bulletin 41, Bureau of American Ethnology*.)

PLATE 13

a. Third story of square tower, showing dado and decoration

b. Deflector and flue of kiva

DETAILS OF CLIFF PALACE

PHOTOGRAPHED BY R. G. FULLER

REFUSE HEAPS

Almost every Mesa Verde cliff-dwelling has an unoccupied space back of the rooms,[28] as in the rear of rooms 28 to 40, which served as a depository for all kinds of rubbish. Here the inhabitants of Cliff Palace also deposited certain of their dead, which became mummified on account of the dryness of the air in the cave.

There is also a vacant space between the rear of the Speaker-chief's House and the cave wall, but this space was almost entirely free of refuse. The amount of débris in the refuse heaps back of the so-called plaza quarter lends weight to other evidence that this is one of the oldest sections of Cliff Palace.

The accumulation of débris was so deep in these places, and the difficulties of removal so great, that it was not attempted. It had all been dug over by relic seekers who are said to have found many specimens therein.[29]

SECULAR ROOMS

The majority of the rooms in Cliff Palace were devoted to secular purposes. These are of several types, and differ in form, in position, and in function. Their form is either circular or rectangular, or some modification of these two. As a rule, the secular rooms lie deep under the cliffs, several extending as far back as the rear of the cave. The front of Cliff Palace shows at least two tiers or terraces of secular rooms, the roof of the lower one being level with that of the floor of the tier above. The front walls of secular rooms lower than the fourth terrace are as a rule destroyed, but the lateral walls are evident, especially in the tower quarter. The passage from one of these terraces to the room above was made by means of ladders or by stone steps along the corners.

The following classification of secular rooms, based on their function, may be noted: (1) Living rooms; (2) milling rooms; (3) storage rooms; (4) rooms of unknown function;[30] (5) towers; (6) round rooms. It is difficult to distinguish in some instances to which of the above classes some of the rooms belong. The secular houses were probably owned by the oldest women of the clan, and the kivas were the property of the men of their respective clans, but courts, plazas, and passageways were common property.

---

[28] Isolated cliff-dwellings are scattered throughout the Southwest, but there are several areas, as the Mesa Verde, in which they are concentrated. Among these clusters may be mentioned the Canyon de Chelly, the Navaho National Monument, the Red Rocks area, and that of the upper Gila. One characteristic feature in which the cliff-dwellings of the Mesa Verde differ from some others is the independence of all of the upright walls from support of the sides of the cliffs. In the cliff-houses of the Navaho Monument a large majority of the houses have the rear wall of the cave as a wall of the building; a few of the houses in Cliff Palace have the same, but the largest number are entirely free from the cliff. This separation on all sides is due largely to the geological structure of the rear of the cavern in which the cliff-house stands.

[29] Workmen could operate in these parts only by tying sponges over their nostrils, so difficult was it to breathe on account of the fine dust.

[30] Possibly some of these may have been used sometimes for ceremonial purposes, or rather for the less important rites.

The masonry[31] of all secular rooms is practically identical and as a rule is inferior to that of kivas, their walls varying in width and having a uniform thickness from foundation to top. There are instances where the lower part projects somewhat beyond the upper, from which it is separated by a ledge, but this feature is not common. Minor features of architecture, as floors and roofs, doors and windows, fireplaces, banks, and cubby-holes, some or all of which may be absent, vary in form and in distribution according to the purpose for which the room was intended. The few timbers that remain show that the beams of the houses were probably cut with stone hatchets aided by the use of fire. The labor of hauling these timbers and of stripping them of their branches must have been great, considering the rude appliances at hand. It would seem that the cliff-dwellers were not ignorant of the use of the wedge with which to split logs, since the surfaces of split sticks are always more or less fibrous, never smooth, as would be expected if metal implements had been used. All transportation was manual, without the assistance of beasts of burden or of any but the rudest mechanical contrivances.

DOORS AND WINDOWS

There is difficulty in distinguishing doorways from windows in cliff-dwellings, on which account they are here treated together. Both are simple openings in the walls, the former as a rule being larger than the latter. As door openings are regularly situated high above the floor, there may have been ladders by which the doorways of the second and third stories were reached. The rooms may have been entered by means of balconies, evidences of which still remain. No instance of a hatchway in the roof is now recognizable, although the absence of side entrances in several rooms implies that there were roof entrances, several good examples of which occur at Spruce-tree House.

Doorways of Cliff Palace have two forms, rectangular and T-shaped, the latter generally opening on the second story or in such a position that they were approached by ladders or notched logs. The theory that these doorways were constructed larger at the top than at the bottom so that persons with packs on their backs might pass through them more readily is not wholly satisfactory, nor does the theory that the notch at the lower rim served to keep the ladder from slipping wholly commend itself. No satisfactory explanation of the form of the T-shaped doorway has been yet determined. Generally the tops of both doorways and windows are narrower than the bottoms, the sides being slightly inclined; but the lower part is rarely narrower than the top. Sills sometimes project slightly, and evidences occur that the sides as well as the upper part of the window and doorway were made of adobe, now no longer in place. The jambs also were probably of clay, and the doors, made of slabs of stone, neatly fitted the orifices.

---

[31] Probably both men and women of one clan worked together in the construction of houses, the men being the masons, the women the plasterers. Each clan built its own rooms, and there were no differentiated groups of mechanics in the community.

PLATE 14

SQUARE TOWER, AFTER REPAIRING

OLD QUARTER

PHOTOGRAPHED BY R. G. FULLER

The prevailing storms in winter at Cliff Palace sweep up the canyon from the southwest, but there does not seem to have been a systematic effort to avoid the cold by placing doors and windows on the opposite side of the building; the openings, for instance, of the Speaker-chief's House face this direction and are open to storms of snow and rain. Many of the openings never had doors and windows, but were probably closed with sticks tied together, or with matting[32]. Certain windows were half closed, probably to temper the winter blasts. The sills of doors were commonly placed a foot or more above the floor[33]; transoms above the door opening and peepholes at the side are not common in Cliff Palace. In some cases a stepping-stone projects from the wall below the door opening to facilitate entrance; in others a foot hole is found in the same relative place.

As the jambs, sills, and lintels were built hard and fast in the mortar, evidently both door openings and windows were constructed when the corresponding wall was built. The jambs in some instances and the lintels in others are of split sticks, the surfaces of which are fibrous and were evidently not split by means of iron implements. There is evidence that the size of the door openings was sometimes reduced by a ridge of mortar which was arched above, as at Spruce-tree House, the intention being to make in this way a jamb to hold in place the stone door. There are no round windows of large size, but both doors and windows are quadrilateral in shape; the small circular openings in some of the walls may have served for lookouts.

FLOORS AND ROOFS

Not a single entire roof remained in Cliff Palace, and only one or two rooms retained remnants of rafters. It would seem, however, from the position of the holes in the walls into which the rafters once extended that they were constructed like those of Spruce-tree House, a good example of which is shown in plate 9 of the report on that ruin. The floors seem to have been formed of clay hardened by tramping, but there is no evidence of paving with flat stones. The hardened adobe is sometimes laid on sticks without bark and stamped down. Although no instance of extensive rock cutting of the floor was observed in secular rooms, this is a common feature of kiva floors. Floors were generally level, but in some instances, when rock was encountered, the surface was raised in part above the other level. The majority of the floors had been dug into for buried specimens before the repair work was begun, but here and there fragments of floors were still intact, showing their former level. Banquettes or ledges around the walls are rare. In a few instances the unplastered roof of the cave served as the roof of the highest rooms.

FIREPLACES

Many fireplaces still remain in rooms, but the majority are found in conve-

---

[32] Some of the doorways were filled with rude masonry; evidently the rooms were thus closed in some instances before the buildings were deserted.

[33] The placing of the sill at a level with the floor is a modern innovation at Walpi. The oldest houses still have it elevated, as in Cliff Palace. In some of the cliff-houses of the Navaho Monument sills and floor levels are continuous.

nient corners of the plazas[34]. The most common situation is in an angle formed by two walls; in which case the fire-pit is generally rimmed with a slightly elevated rounded ridge of adobe. In room 84 there is a fireplace in the middle of the floor. At one side of this depression there extends a supplementary groove in the floor, rimmed with stone, the use of which is not known. Although fireplaces are ordinarily half round, a square one occurs in the northwestern corner of room 81. All the fireplaces contained wood ashes, sometimes packed hard; but no cinders, large fragments of charcoal, or coal ashes were evident. The sides of the walls above the fireplaces are generally blackened with smoke.

The fire-holes of the kivas, being specially constructed, are different in shape from those in secular houses. While the cooking fire-pits are generally shallow, kiva fire-holes a foot deep are not exceptional, and several are much deeper. The fire was kindled in the kiva not so much for heating the room, as for lighting it, there being no windows for that purpose. Certain kinds of fuel were probably prescribed, but logs were not burned in kivas on account of the heat. No evidences of smoke-hoods or chimneys have been found in any of the Cliff Palace rooms. The walls of many kivas showed blackening by soot or smoke.

LIVING ROOMS

It is difficult to distinguish rooms in which the inhabitants lived from others used by them for storage and other purposes, since most of their work, as cooking, pottery making, and like domestic operations, was conducted either on the house-tops or in the plazas. Under living rooms are included the women's rooms[35], or those in which centered the family life; and, in a general way, we may suppose the large rooms and those with banquettes were sleeping rooms. The popular misconception that the cliff-dwellers were of small stature has undoubtedly arisen from the diminutive size of all the secular rooms, but it must be remembered that the life of the cliff-dwellers was really an out-of-door one, the roof of the cave affording the necessary protection.

---

[34] Smoke on the walls of certain second and third stories shows that fireplaces were not restricted to the ground floor.

[35] Among the Hopi the oldest woman, as a clan representative, owns the living rooms, but kivas are the property of the men, the kiva chief of certain fraternities being the direct descendant of the clan chief of the ceremony when limited to his clan.

PLATE 15

SPEAKER-CHIEF'S HOUSE, AFTER REPAIRING

PHOTOGRAPHED BY R. G. FULLER

MILLING ROOMS

There are several rooms in Cliff Palace which appear to have been given up solely to the operation of grinding corn. The mills are box-like structures, constructed of slabs of stone set on edge, each containing a slanting stone called a metate, from which the mill is called by the Hopi the *metataki*, or "metate house." The following description of a metataki in pueblos seen by Castañeda in 1540 applies, in a general way, to the small milling troughs in Cliff Palace:

> One room is appointed for culinary purposes, another for the grinding of corn; the latter is isolated [not so in Cliff Palace] and contains an oven and three stones [one, two, three, or four in Cliff Palace], cemented finely together. Three women sit [kneel] before these stones; the first crushes the corn, the second grinds it, and the third reduces it quite to a powder.

In grinding corn, which was generally the work of the girls or young women, the grinder knelt before the metataki and used a flat stone, which was rubbed back and forth on the metate. The corn meal thus ground fell into a squarish depression, made of smooth stones, at the lower end of the metate. Commonly the corners of this receptacle for the meal that had been ground were filled in with clay, and on each side of the metate were inserted fragments of pottery, which rounded the corners and made it easier to brush the meal into a heap. In room 92, where there are four metates, occupying almost the whole milling room, there are upright stones on the side of the wall, back of the place where the women knelt, against which they braced their feet.

Most of the grinding boxes were destroyed, but those in the Speaker-chief's house and others west of kiva V, especially the latter, were still in good condition, the metates being in place. Evidences of former metatakis were apparent in the floor of several other rooms, as in a room back of kiva K. It is evident from the number of metates found in Cliff Palace that several milling rooms, not now recognizable, formerly existed, and it is probable that every large clan had its own milling room, with, one or more metatakis, according to necessity. Although, many metates without metatakis occur in Cliff Palace, that in itself is not evidence that they were moved from place to place by the inhabitants. These milling rooms were apparently roofed, low, and one-storied, possibly in some instances open on top, but generally had a small peephole or window for the entrance of light or for permitting the grinders to see passers-by.

GRANARIES

Under the general name of granaries are included storage rooms, some of which are situated below living rooms.[36] Here corn for consumption was stacked, and if we may follow Hopi customs in our interpretation of cliff-dwellers' habits, the people of Cliff Palace no doubt had a supply sufficient to prevent famine

---

[36] Genetically the room for storage of property was of earliest construction. This custom, which was necessary among agriculturists whose food supply was bulky, may have led to the choice of caves, natural or artificial, for habitation.

by tiding over a failure of crops for two or more years. Many of these chambers were without doorways or windows; they were not limited to storage of corn, but served for the preservation of any food products or valuable cult paraphernalia. Each clan no doubt observed more or less secrecy in the amount of corn it kept for future use, and on that account the storage rooms were ordinarily, hidden from view.

The droppings of chipmunks and other rodents show that these commensals were numerous, and their presence made necessary the building of storage rooms in such manner that they would be proof against the ravages of such animals. The three cists constructed of stone slabs placed vertically, situated back of the Speaker-chief's House, sometimes called "eagle houses," were probably storage bins; in support of this hypothesis may be mentioned the fact that the cobs, tassels, and leaves of corn are said to have been abundant in them when Cliff Palace was first visited by white men.

Although eagle bones are found in the refuse in the unoccupied part of the cave back of the houses, their abundance does not necessarily prove that eagles were confined in them by the inhabitants of Cliff Palace. Perhaps the eagle nests in the canyon were owned by different clans and were visited yearly or whenever feathers were needed, and the dead eagles were probably buried ceremonially in these places, which therefore may be called eagle cemeteries, as among the Hopi.[37]

CREMATORIES

As is well known to students of the Southwest, the tribes of Indians dwelling along the lower Colorado river disposed of their dead by cremation, and evidences of burning the dead are found among all the ruins along the Gila and Salt rivers in southern Arizona. The custom was also practiced in the San Pedro and Salt River valleys, and along other tributaries of the Gila river. Castañeda (1540) says that the inhabitants of Cibola, identified with Zuñi, burned their dead, but no indication of this practice is now found among existing Pueblos. The ancient Pueblo inhabitants of the Little Colorado, so far as known, did not burn their dead, and no record has been made of the practice among their descendants, the Hopi and Zuñi.

---

[37] See Property Rights in Eagles, *American Anthropologist*, vol. ii, pp. 690-707, 1907.

**NORTHERN PART, FROM THE SPEAKER-CHIEF'S HOUSE TO THE WEST-
ERN END**

In his excellent work on the ruins of the Mesa Verde, Baron Nordenskiöld speaks of calcined human bones being found in a stone cist at Step House, and Mr. Wetherill is referred to as having observed evidence of cremation elsewhere among the Mesa Verde cliff-dwellings. There can be no doubt from the observations made in the refuse heaps at Cliff Palace that the inhabitants of this village not only burned their dead but there was a special room in the depths of the cave which was set aside for that purpose.[38] One of these rooms, situated at the northern end of the refuse heap, was excavated in the progress of the work and found to contain bushels of very fine phosphate ashes, mixed with fragments of bones, some of which are well enough preserved to enable their identification as human. Accompanying these calcined bones were various mortuary objects not unlike those occurring in graves where the dead were not cremated. The existence of great quantities of ashes, largely containing phosphates, apparently derived from the burned bones, forming much of the refuse, and the densely smoke-blackened roof of the cave above them, are interpreted to indicate that the dead were cremated in the cave back of the houses.

In addition to these burning places, or crematories, in the rear of the buildings of Cliff Palace, there is good evidence of the same practice on the mesa top. Here and there, especially in the neighborhood of the clearings where the cliff-dwellers formerly had their farms, are round stone inclosures, oftentimes several feet deep, in which occur great quantities of bone ashes, fragments of pottery, and some stone objects. The surface of the stones composing these inclosures shows the marks of intense fire, which, taken in connection with the existence of fragments of human bones more or less burned, indicate that the dead were cremated in these inclosures. It is not clear, however, that the dead were not interred before cremation, and there is reason for believing that the bodies were dried before they were committed to the flames. The mortuary offerings, especially pottery, seem to have been placed in the burning places after the heat had subsided, for beautiful jars showing no action of fire were found in some of these inclosures. The existence of cremation among the cliff-dwellers is offered as an explanation of the great scarcity of skeletons in their neighborhood. When it is remembered that Cliff Palace must have had a population of several hundred, judging from the number of the buildings, and was inhabited for several generations, it otherwise would be strange that so few skeletons were found. It would appear that the chiefs or the priestly class were buried either in the ground or in the floors of the rooms, which were afterward sealed, whereas the bodies of the poorer class, or the people generally, were cremated. The former existence of Pueblo peoples who buried their dead in the region between the Gila valley and Mesa Verde where the dead were cremated is a significant fact, but further observations are necessary before it can be interpreted. It may be that in ancient times all the sedentary tribes practiced cremation, and that the region in question was settled after this custom had been abandoned.

LEDGE ROOMS

In a shallow crevice in the roof of the cave on a higher level than the roofs of the tallest houses there is a long wall, the front of inclosures that may be called

[38] While only one place where bodies were burned was found in Cliff Palace, several such places were found on top of the mesa. Evidences of similar inclosures occur at Sprucetree House and at Step House.

"ledge rooms."[39] Some of these rooms have plastered walls, others are roughly laid; the latter form one side of a court and served to shield those passing from one room to another. On this outer wall, about midway, there is painted in white an inverted terrace figure, which may represent a rain cloud. Attention should be called to the resemblance in form and position of this figure to that on an outside wall overlooking plaza C of Spruce-tree House. This series of ledge rooms was probably entered from the roof of a building in front, and the opening or doorway above room 66 served as such an entrance, according to several stockmen who visited Cliff Palace in earlier days.

---

[39] This type of building is believed to be the oldest in those sections of the Southwest where cliff habitations occur.

ENUMERATION OF THE ROOMS
IN CLIFF PALACE

SECULAR ROOMS

The rooms in Cliff Palace, now numbered from 1 to 94, include all those on the ground floor, but do not embrace the second, third, and fourth stories nor the elevated ledge rooms secluded in the crevices of the cave roof at a high level. Their classification by function already having been considered, a brief enumeration by form and other characters will be given.

Room 1, situated at the extreme southern end, presents no striking features except that one of its entrances is by stairs through the floor from kiva A. Its western and northern walls are of masonry; the remaining sides are formed by the vertical cliff.

The walls of room 2 are constructed of masonry on the northern, western, and southern sides; the eastern side is the cliff face. As the floor of this room is made of hardened clay laid on small sticks, it was at first supposed that a human burial was concealed beneath, but excavation showed no signs of an interment.

Room 3 (pl. 17) is a square inclosure between walls of other rooms. A portion of its floor is level with that of rooms 1 and 2, but a projecting rock forms an elevated bench on the eastern side. On the underside of this rock there are pictographs, apparently aboriginal, one of which has a well-known terrace form, recalling the outlines of a T-shaped doorway and the white figures on the outer wall of the ledge room above mentioned.

Room 4 is three stories high, without openings into adjoining rooms or exterior entrances. Its western corner is rounded below and angular above.

Room 5 was apparently two stories high, with a fireplace in its southeastern corner. The foundation rests on a large rock. The arrangement of post holes in the south and west walls of this dwelling is exceptional, and their purpose enigmatical. There is a passage from room 5 to the neighboring plaza, which is occupied by kiva D.

Room 6 is a small rectangular chamber, about 2 feet square and 7 feet high; it has an entrance on the western side into room 7, and, as it utilizes the walls of the adjacent rooms, it was doubtless built subsequent to them. Evidences of rebuilding or secondary construction of walls on old foundations are so numerous in this section of the ruin that this may be the oldest part of Cliff Palace.

PLATE 17

a. Tunnel to Kiva B

b. Passageway with steps to room 3

DETAILS OF KIVA A

PHOTOGRAPHED BY R. G. FULLER

Rooms 7, 8, and 9 are outside rooms, the western walls of which are more or less broken, while the front is entirely destroyed. It appears that their connected roofs once formed a terrace overlooking kiva D on the west. There are doorways in walls of one of these rooms, but entrance may have been gained by means of hatchways. It was approached from plaza B by the aid of ladders or stone steps.

Room 11, which may be called the square tower, is the only four-story building standing in Cliff Palace, its walls reaching from the floor to the roof of the cave. When work began on this building the whole northwestern angle had fallen, and the remaining walls were tottering. To prevent total destruction, the entire corner was built up from a foundation laid on the floor level of the neighboring kiva. A small entrance to the ground floor, or the lowest of the four rooms, is from a banquette (10) on the western side, where there is a passageway from this lower story of room 11 to room 12, situated in its rear. Room 12 has a good floor, and room 11 a fireplace in the southwestern corner of the lowest room of the square tower. Almost all the beams of the higher rooms of this tower had been taken out, leaving nothing but the holes in the walls to indicate the former existence of floors. The beams now connecting the walls were placed there by our workmen to serve as staging and for tying the sides together. The second and third stories of the square tower are also without floors. Their inner walls are plastered a reddish color, in places whitewashed, and the third wall is decorated with interesting paintings. In the western wall of the second story was a small window, and portions of a large T-shaped doorway still show on the northern wall of the third story. Split sticks support the section of wall from the top of this doorway to the roof of the cave. From the arrangement of its rear walls it would appear that the whole of this tower was built subsequently to the rooms back of it, which extend on each side, north and south. The repair of a doorway of the northern wall was difficult, the foundation walls of the eastern and northern corners of the tower being slabs of stone set on edge, quite inadequate to support the lofty wall above. This insufficient foundation leads to the belief that when the base of the square tower was constructed there was no thought of erecting upon it the four stories that we now find. (Pl. 12, 13*a*, 14*a*.)

Some of the rooms of the square tower bear evidence of having been living rooms, and possibly the approaches to the upper chambers were by ladders from the outside; otherwise the T-shaped doorway on the northern side, above the painted room, remains unexplained.

Room 12, situated east of the square tower, has no characteristic features, being more a passageway than a room, opening at one end into room 13 and connecting with kiva D at the other end.

Room 13 likewise presents no distinctive features; its rear wall is considerably blackened by smoke, and it has a large square window opening into room 12.

PLATE 18

KIVA H, BEFORE REPAIRING

PHOTOGRAPHED BY R. G. FULLER

A large part of the front walls of rooms 14, 16, and 24 has fallen, having been destroyed by falling water. To obviate future destruction, the southwestern corner of room 16 was repaired with cement, thus preventing further harm from dripping water. Rooms 16 and 24 evidently formed a front terrace, perhaps one story high, their rear wall being the front wall of rooms 17 and 18.

Rooms 17 and 18 are of two stories; both are square. The upper part of its walls shows that a portion of room 18 was formerly one story high and that the walls were erected before those of room 17. A coping of masonry around three walls is a feature of room 18, the construction of which is superior to that of room 17. This room has a large front window and two smaller openings higher up in the second story of the western wall. The combined front walls of rooms 17 and 18 may be ranked among the finest examples of masonry in Cliff Palace. The large embrasures made in this wall by vandals were repaired.

Rooms 19 and 20 also present fine examples of masonry and were evidently constructed before rooms 21, 22, and 23. The inner walls of room 19 were plastered; the outer wall was left rough. Room 20 shows crude masonry; its rear wall is the vertical cliff, and the inner surfaces of the three remaining walls of the upper story were plastered, and painted with yellow sand or pigment. Apparently the lower room was used as a granary, having no entrance, except possibly through a hatchway in its roof, which forms the floor of the room above. The presence of sticks projecting from the walls of this room adds weight to the conclusion that it was used for storage. There is no indication of a fireplace.

Room 22 has a stepping-stone, which may have facilitated entrance, projecting from the wall under an opening that probably served as a doorway.

Room 23 has a fireplace in one corner, and rooms 25, 26, and 27, which are situated in a row, have for their rear wall the vertical face of the cliff. Although these rooms are only one story high, the roof of the cave slopes down low enough in the rear to form their roofs. The outer walls were plastered, and each room was entered by a separate doorway. Although their side walls were somewhat destroyed, they appear not to have been intercommunicating. It is, in fact, rare to find a doorway from one room into another on the same level, or suites of rooms communicating with one another, but chambers one above another are generally provided with hatchways.

Room 28 is a two-story structure of excellent masonry, with an entrance on its southern side and a window frame of stone. Its second story formerly opened on the western side into room 29. Not much now remains of the plastering that once covered the inner walls of room 28, but the interior walls of room 29 still show well-preserved plaster. Although the latter room has excellent masonry, its southern wall, or that facing kiva J, is entirely destroyed. The floor was so well preserved that but little work was required to put it in good condition.

Rooms 30 to 33 are represented almost entirely by the side walls, the front walls being more or less destroyed. Their floors lie on the same level as those of the second terrace, and their roofs may have been continuous with the third terrace. There is indication of a room (unnumbered) in the southwestern corner of plaza J, and another, too mutilated to be described, on the second terrace below it.

Room 34 is irregularly rectangular in shape; its floor is on the level of the roof of kiva H. It has good masonry and a smoothed stone sill with a groove cut in the upper surface for the slab that formed the door. Its interior walls show evidences of plastering.

Room 35, situated on the same level as the kiva roof, has no window, but there is an opening directly into kiva H. Its roof is a continuation of that of the kiva, and has the old rafters, some still in place, supporting a few of the flat stones which formed the upper walls. As this chamber opens directly into the kiva, we may regard it as a repository for kiva paraphernalia;[40] the Hopi designate a similar chamber *Katcinakihu*, "Katcina house." On the roof of this room the writer set in place a smooth, ovoid stone with flat base, artificially worked. Possibly this stone was formerly used as an idol.

In Hano, a pueblo on the East mesa of the Hopi, masks are kept in a special room back of a living room, a custom common to all the Hopi. There is no evidence that the Cliff Palace people performed masked dances.

The most picturesque building of Cliff Palace is the round tower, room 36, perched on a high rock overlooking kivas G and H. From it the observer may have a fine view of the entire ruin and the canyon, especially the view down the latter, which is unsurpassed. This tower is not unlike other towers in the San Juan and Mesa Verde regions, one of the most perfect of which is that in Navaho canyon, repeatedly figured. This prominent tower is built of worked stones laid in reddish mortar, and apparently was plastered both inside and outside. It is two stories high, but is without a floor in the upper story, or a roof. The theory in certain quarters that this round tower formerly extended to the roof of the cave is not accepted by the author, who believes that it was formerly only a few feet higher than at present. The break in the upper wall adds much to its picturesque character, which is likewise increased by its association with neighboring buildings. The round tower has a doorway in its lower story, and above is another smaller opening, possibly a window. Several small peepholes are present on the western side. The sides of this structure are symmetrical, its walls slanting gradually inward from the base upward, and its vertical lines curving slightly on the western side. (Pl. 4a, 11.)

Room 37 is a well-preserved room with a metataki, or grinding bin, in the middle.

While rooms 38 and 39 appear to be living rooms, they present no special peculiarities. The northern wall of room 39 was wholly undermined and tottering when the work of repair was commenced, so that its foundations had to be built up from the floor of kiva M. To make this difficult repair work effective it was necessary to enlarge the base of the wall, making the side of kiva M curve slightly

---

[40] The Mongkiva at Walpi has such a chamber which is closed by a door and is opened only when paraphernalia for certain ceremonies are desired. In the Warrior House at Walpi there is a similar chamber, ordinarily closely sealed, in which the fetishes of the Warrior Society are kept. Masked dancers among the Pueblos are called Katcinas, and the masks they wear would naturally be kept in a house (*kihu*) called "Katcinakihu."

inward and thereby insuring a good foundation.

PLATE 19

SOUTHEASTERN WALL OF KIVA Q, BEFORE REPAIRING

PHOTOGRAPHED BY F. K. VREELAND

The walls of rooms 41 and 42 are well preserved; the top of the cave served as the roof. These rooms were entered from the plaza containing kiva M. In room

42 a stepping-stone is set in the outer wall below the doorway, the object being to facilitate entrance. It is said that this room, the roof of which shows signs of smoke, was occupied by campers while engaged in rifling the ruin of its contents.

The cluster of rooms numbered 43 to 45 have well-constructed walls, but they have been considerably mutilated. Pegs from which, no doubt, objects were formerly hung, project from the smoothly plastered interior walls of one of these rooms.

Rooms 47 and 48 show the holes of floor joists, so placed as to indicate two stories. These rooms form the southern side of the court, which extends from the main plaza of the settlement to the round rooms at the northern extremity. In front of room 50 there is a low platform from which one steps into the room through an entrance situated about midway of its length.

Room 51 has a very well preserved fireplace in the northwestern corner and a doorway about midway in the northern wall. Its well-plastered walls show impressions of the hands and fingers of the plasterers.

The eastern side of the "street"[41] is bordered by rooms 60 to 63, inclusive, which open into it. In the wall of the last room (61) to the south there is a small peephole that enabled the owners to see from within the room anyone entering the street from the court. Room 59, probably the largest angular room in Cliff Palace, is without an entrance. Its high walls form a part of the northern and eastern ends of the court and almost the whole western side of the street. A large embrasure in its southern wall had been repaired by the ancient masons before Cliff Palace was deserted. North of room 59 remains of the foundations of rooms (not numbered on the plan) were found, and it may be possible that at this point there was a small open space, without a kiva; if so, it would have been exceptional in Cliff Palace.

Rooms 66 and 68 are round rooms, not kivas, although possibly ceremonial in character. From the roof of room 66, the walls of which are now lower than formerly, it was possible to pass on a level into one of the series of ledge rooms previously described. The floor of room 68 is exceptional in being lower than that of the cave outside, so that on entering it one descends by a step or two. Room 67 appears to have been more a passageway (*kisombi*) than a room, a step from it leading down to the level of the triangular plaza in front of the Speaker-chief's House, south of room 70.

Room 70 is a milling room, with two well-preserved metatakis in one corner, each with a set of metates. In the wall above these mealing troughs there is a small window through which the women engaged in grinding corn could see the passers through the court east of this room. The opposite corner is occupied by a fireplace, and the adjacent wall is pierced by a doorway with elevated threshold, through which one passed from the milling room to the broad Speaker-chief's platform south of rooms 71 and 72.

The inclosed space west of rooms 71 and 73 is separated from the rear of the cave by a high wall which shuts off entrance on this side. The series of rooms numbered 71 to 74, and the two rooms west of these, form, with the banquette

[41] A passage or inclosure surrounded by high walls is called kisombi by the Hopi.

and the neighboring plaza, what is here arbitrarily designated the Speaker-chief's House, the walls of which consist of some of the finest masonry in Cliff Palace. It is protected on the western side by a high, well-plastered wall extending southward from the corner of room 72, so placed as to shield the plaza from storms from this side. The banquette south of rooms 72 and 73 is also finely plastered, and is approached from the plaza by a single step. This banquette probably was designed for the use of the Speaker-chief, but a similar structure on the eastern side of the plaza quarter served another purpose.

The masonry, the doors and windows, and other structural features of the Speaker-chief's House are the best in Cliff Palace. Lintels, jambs, and door and window sills are of smooth-dressed stones and project beyond the wall. The rear rooms of this cluster extend to the roof of the cave, being three stories high, while those in front are two stories in height. The line of holes shown in plate 15 indicates the former position of rafters, but all signs of woodwork have disappeared from this section of the ruin.

On the western side of the Speaker-chief's House are two rooms, 79 and 80, likewise well built. The former has a banquette extending across the eastern side, and the latter is triangular in shape, with the exterior side rounded. The foundations of these rooms rest upon a large rock that has settled and cracked, the crack extending vertically into the walls, showing that it has developed since the wall was constructed.

The inclosures 76 to 78, extending to the cave roof, are more like granaries for the storage of corn. They are built of flat stone slabs placed on edge, and rest on bowlders that have fallen from the cave roof, which is here lower than in the middle part of the cavern. Of these inclosures, 78 is the best preserved, all holes in its angles being skillfully closed with adobe mortar, so that even now if the door were replaced it would be almost rat proof. The door opening is square, and is situated at the western side. There is no adequate evidence that these rooms served as turkey houses, as some have interpreted them.

PLATE 20

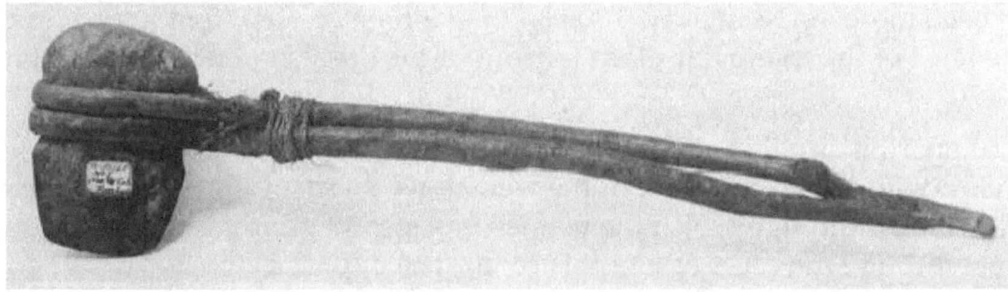

AXE WITH ORIGINAL HANDLE

The rear walls of rooms 89 and 90 are well preserved, but those in front have been completely destroyed. The former has a banquette like that of the Speaker-chief's House. The walls of rooms situated north and east of kiva U, now reduced in height, formerly extended to the roof of the cave, which is here somewhat lower than in the middle of the cavern. The existence of these former walls is indicated by light bands on the smoke-covered surface of the cave roof, and fragments of clay still adhering to the side of the cliff show that the walls here were two and three stories high.

In rooms 84, 85, and 86 the builder took advantage of the cliff for rear walls. The middle of the floor of 84 has a depression lined with vertical slabs of stone, evidently a fireplace, as it contained a quantity of wood ashes. In the floor on the eastern side of this fireplace there is a short trench also lined with stone and containing wood ashes, the relation of which to the other inclosure is unknown. It appears that this exceptional structure was not used in the same way as the fireplaces so constantly met with in other rooms, but that it might have been used for baking paper-bread, called *piki* by the Hopi. In a corner of room 91 there is another depression, half under the floor, covered with a flat stone, that appears quite likely to have been used for this purpose. Unlike the fireplaces sunken in the floor, the one in room 84 is partially or wholly above the floor, its confining stones being several inches above the floor level.

Room 92 is the best example of a milling room in Cliff Palace. It has four grinding bins, or metatakis, arranged side by side, with all the parts entire and in working condition. When excavation was begun in this part of the ruin these structures were wholly concealed under fallen rocks. As streams of water from a vertical cleft in the cliff poured down upon them after exposure during periods of rain, it was necessary to construct a roof to protect them.[42] The discovery of this and of other grinding rooms shows that the cliff-house metatakis are the same in structure as those in the Hopi pueblos. In an inclosure south of these metatakis was found a granary. Fragments of walls projecting from the cliff west of room 93 show the former existence of rooms in this section, but as their front walls have been obliterated by the downpour of water their form is obscure.

KIVAS

There are in Cliff Palace 23 ceremonial rooms that may be called kivas.[43] These consist of two types: (1) generally circular or cylindrical subterranean rooms, with pilasters to support the roof, and with fireplace, deflector, and ventilator. (2) Cir-

---

[42] On the top of the rock that forms the foundation of the walls of these rooms, and south of them, are hollows or grooves where the metates were ground, and shallow pits used in some prehistoric game. There are similar pits in some of the kiva floors.

[43] The word *kiva*, now universally employed in place of the Spanish designation "estufa" to designate a ceremonial room of the Pueblos, is derived from the Hopi language. The designation is archaic, the element ki being both Pima and Hopi for "house." It has been sought to connect this word with a part of the human body, and esoterically the kiva represents one of the underworlds or womb of the earth from which the races of man were born. It is highly appropriate that ancient ceremonies should take place in a kiva, the symbolic representation of an underworld, for many of the ceremonies are said to have been practiced while man still lived within the Earth Mother. The word *kiva* is restricted to subterranean chambers, rectangular or circular, in which secret ceremonies are or were held, and the term *kihu* is suggested for ceremonial rooms above ground. The five kivas at Walpi are examples of the true kiva, while the Flute chamber may be called a *kihu*.

cular or rectangular rooms with rounded corners, without pilasters, fireplace, or deflector. In the first group may be placed provisionally a subtype (kiva M, for example), without pilasters but with a single large banquette. As this subtype is the dominant one in the western part of the San Juan drainage, it may be necessary later to regard it as a type. As a rule rooms of the second type are not subterranean, but are commonly surrounded by high walls, being entered by a doorway at one side. There are 20 rooms pertaining to the first type and three to the second type in Cliff Palace.[44]

The majority of the kivas are situated in front of the secular buildings, but several are in the rear of the cave, with high rooms in front of them. The largest cluster of kivas on the cave floor lies in the so-called plaza quarter, which takes its name from the open space occupied by the kivas in that section. The rooms on the terraces, especially those near the southern end of the ruin, were covered with fallen rocks and other débris when the excavation and repair work began. The walls of most of the kivas, whether in front or in the rear, were greatly dilapidated and in all instances it was necessary to rebuild them to the level of the plazas in which the kivas are situated.

Following comparisons with modern pueblos, there is every reason to suppose that the kivas preserve the oldest types of buildings of the cliff-dweller culture, and it is believed that the form of these archaic structures is a survival of antecedent conditions. They belonged to the men of different clans, as in a measure is the case among the Hopi at the present day, with whom every kiva is spoken of as that of a certain man who is a clan chief. The male and female members of every Hopi clan have affiliation with certain kivas (a survival of archaic conditions), and in certain clan gatherings, as the dramatic exhibition which occurs in March, the celebration takes place in their respective kivas.

As the kiva is the men's room, and as religious exercises are largely controlled by men, such ceremonies occur in kivas, which are practically the ceremonial rooms.[45]

KIVAS OF THE FIRST TYPE

All kivas of the first type are constructed on the same general plan, the different parts being somewhat modified by surrounding conditions. While their general form is circular or cylindrical, some are square with rounded angles, others oblong, and others more or less heart-shaped. Their diameter and height vary according to circumstances, but this type is always subterranean when possible, even though excavation in the rock may be necessary.

The walls of the kivas are sometimes double, and the masonry is generally well constructed. The walls show evidences of plastering, which is decorated in some instances with paintings or incised figures. The number of pilasters is commonly 6, but 4 and 8 are also evident; rarely, as in kiva M (the subtype), all are

---

[44] The so-called "warrior room" in Spruce-tree House belongs to the second type.

[45] In certain ceremonies of Hopi women's societies the kiva has also come to be a meeting place for these sororities and where they erect their altars.

missing. Between these pilasters are the so-called banquettes, one of which is usually larger than the others. The banquettes are generally built 3 or 4 feet in height, consequently they could scarcely have been intended for seats.

PLATE 21

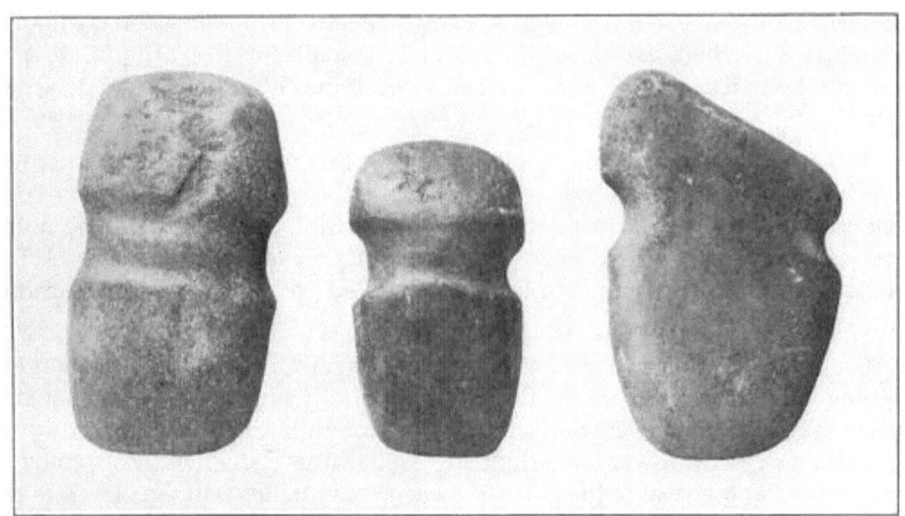

STONE HATCHETS

The pilasters are commonly rectangular, sometimes square, the size being about uniform from base upward. In rare instances a pilaster has a cubby-hole[46]

---

[46] These small holes, generally square, are usually found in the wall below the ban-

in one side. Where circumstances require the ventilator penetrates the rear portion of the pilaster, but the flue never enters the side of the kiva under a pilaster.

The pilasters, which are almost universal in kivas of the first type, as has been shown in the description and illustrations of the eight kivas of Spruce-tree House, served as supports for the roof beams. These rafters of pine rested upon and served to support other logs laid one over another, so that finally the roof opening was covered. Across the middle of the walls, at the top, two long parallel logs were placed, in order to add stability to the roof structure. These beams were set far enough apart to allow a hatch midway between their ends, which served the purpose of an entrance and also permitted the escape of smoke from the fire directly below.

Over the framework of logs were laid small sticks, filling the interstices, and above these was spread a layer of cedar bark; the whole was then covered with clay, thus bringing the upper surface of the roof to the level of the adjacent plaza. Whether the kiva walls projected above the plaza and roof level is unknown, but possibly they did, and there may have been a slight elevation of the hatchway, as in the Hopi kivas. It is commonly believed that the kiva roof was level with the surrounding plaza and that the entrance was through a hatchway, but no depression or other sign of a ladder or of its resting place on the kiva floor has yet been found in any of the Mesa Verde ruins.

The floors of the kivas are commonly of hardened adobe; unlike those of the Hopi kivas they are never paved with stones, but the natural rock often serves for that purpose. It is not rare to find the surface of solid rock that forms the kiva floor cut down a few feet to a lower level. Although generally smooth, when the floor is the natural rock there are sometimes found in it small, cup-like, artificial depressions similar to those in the horizontal surfaces of the cliff or in slabs of detached rock.

The fire-pit, which is found in all kivas of the first type,[47] is a circular depression situated slightly to one side of the middle of the room. While generally lined with adobe, slabs of stone sometimes form its border, and it is also to be noted that one or two of these small stones sometimes project above the floor level. The fire-hole is sometimes deep, and is generally filled with wood ashes, indicating long use.

Every kiva of the first type has a lateral passageway for the admission of air, opening into the chamber on the floor level, generally under the large banquette. This passage, or tunnel, here designated a flue, communicates either directly with the outside or turns upward at a right angle and forms a small vertical ventilator which opens at the level of the plaza. Between the entrance into the flue from the

---

quette.

[47] The fire in these rooms was more for light than for heat, for when roofed a large fire would have produced so much smoke and heat that the occupants would be driven out. The character of the ashes indicates that logs were not used as firewood, but that the prescribed kiva fuel was, as at Walpi, small twigs or brush. No evidence of lamps has been found in cliff-dwellings, the lamp-shaped pottery objects having been used for purposes other than illumination.

kiva and the fire-hole there rises from the floor a device called the deflector (sometimes called an altar), the object of which was to prevent flames and smoke being drawn into the ventilator, or to evenly circulate the inflowing fresh air in the chamber. This deflector may be (1) a low stone wall, free on both ends; (2) a curved wall connected with the kiva wall on each side with orifices to allow the passage of air; (3) a stone slab in the kiva floor; (4) a bank, free at each end, supported by upright stakes between which are woven twigs, the whole being plastered with clay.[48]

PLATE 22

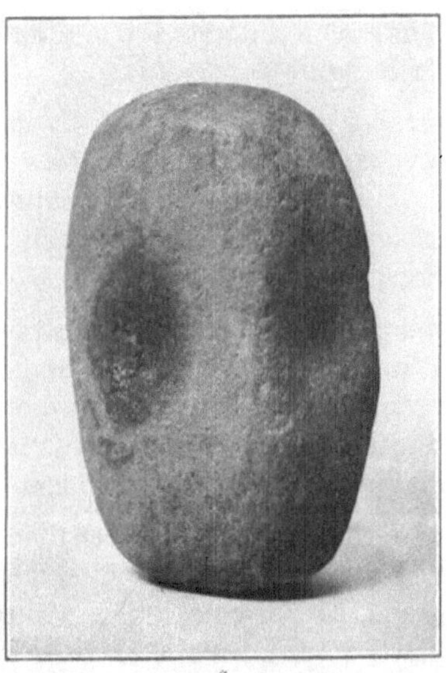

STONE OBJECTS

a. Pounding stone, b. Projectile point, c. Cover for vase, d. Flat stone slab

[48] Cosmos Mindeleff quotes from Nordenskiöld a description of a Mesa Verde kiva, the deflector of which was made in the same way.

The supposed functions of the flue, the vertical passage, and the ventilator have been discussed by several archeologists. The uses to which the flue has been ascribed are as follows: (1) a chimney, (2) a ceremonial opening, (3) an entrance, (4) a ventilator. There is no sign of smoke on the interior of the vertical passage, which, being too small to admit a person, would seem to prove the first and third theories untenable. In the Navaho National Monument, where there are square rooms, or *kihus*, with banks similar to the deflectors of the circular kivas, a door takes the place of the flue and the vertical passage, and affords the only means for admitting fresh air to the room. Although it may have originated as a simple entrance to the room, it became so modified that it could no longer have served that purpose, ceremonially or otherwise.

The position of the entrance to the Cliff Palace kiva is yet to be definitely determined. Analogy, together with the structure of the roof, would indicate that it was by means of a hatchway, but no remains of a ladder were found, and no indication in the floor where a ladder formerly rested is visible. It may be that the large banquette indicates the position of the hatchway.[49]

The subterranean passageway under the flue and beneath the floor of kiva V should not be overlooked in a study of the origin and function of the ventilator. This structure is without apparent connection with the ventilator, and yet it is so carefully constructed under it that it may have had some relation, a knowledge of which will eventually enlighten us regarding the meaning of both structures.

The kivas of the Mesa Verde are much smaller than those of Walpi and other Hopi pueblos, one of them being barely 9 feet in diameter and the largest measuring not more than 19 feet, whereas the chief kiva at Walpi is 25 feet long by 15 feet wide. Evidently kivas of such diminutive size as those found at Cliff Palace could accommodate only a few at a time, and it is probable that they were not occupied by fraternities of priests but by a few chiefs; indeed, the religious fraternity, as we understand its composition in modern pueblos, had in all probability not yet been developed. Nevertheless the smallest kiva in Cliff Palace is as large as the room in Walpi in which the Sun priests, mainly of one clan, celebrate their rites.

Kiva A

Kiva A (pl. 17) is the most southerly kiva of Cliff Palace, the first of the series excavated in the talus, its roof having been on the level of the cave floor, or the fourth terrace. The walls of this kiva required little repair. Its height from the floor to the top of the walls is 8 feet 6 inches, and from the floor to the top of the pilasters 7 feet; the height of the banquette is 3 feet 6 inches. The interior diameter is 11 feet. There are six pilasters, with an average breadth of 20 inches; the distance between them averages 4 feet 6 inches.

The opening into the ventilator is situated in the southwestern wall; its height is 2 feet 4 inches, the breadth, at the base, 14 inches, contracted to 11 inches at the top. The deflector, which is broken, is a thin slab of stone. The distance from the flue opening to the deflector is 2 feet 6 inches, and from the deflector to the round

[49] On this supposition the large banquette may have been the forerunner of the spectator's section in the modern rectangular Hopi kivas, of which it is a modification.

fire-hole 8 inches. The diameter of the fire-hole is 1 foot 8 inches, its depth 2 feet. Its western side is lined with small stones set on edge.

There were possibly 4 niches in the side wall of the banquette, 3 of them on the east, measuring respectively 16 by 20 by 12 inches, 9 by 9 by 12 inches, and 3 by 3 by 5 inches, and the remaining one situated north by east from the middle of the kiva and measuring 6 by 4 by 8 inches.[50]

There is a subterranean passageway (pl. 17, *b*), 6 feet 6 inches long, from this kiva into room 1, and also a tunnel (pl. 17, *a*), 6 feet in length, between kivas A and B. The former has stone steps and rises above the banquette; its width averages 18 inches.

Kiva B

Kiva B adjoins kiva A, and is the second of the terraced rooms, its roof being originally on the same level as the former. It is circular in shape, and the height from the floor to the top of the room is 9 feet 6 inches. The height of the top of the pilasters from the floor is 7 feet, and that of the banquette 3 feet 6 inches.

The inner diameter of the kiva is 13 feet 6 inches. There are 6 pilasters, averaging 2 feet in width. The position of the ventilator opening is south by west; its depth 4 feet, and height 2 feet 6 inches. The breadth of this opening at the top (it narrows somewhat at the base) is 18 inches.

The deflector[51] is a slab of stone about 3 feet 10 inches wide. The distance from the deflector to the kiva wall is 2 feet 6 inches, and from the deflector to the fire-hole 14 inches. The diameter of the fire-hole measures 2 feet, and its depth 9 inches. The distance from the ceremonial opening, or sipapû, to the fire-hole is 4 feet. The diameter of the sipapû is 4 inches and its depth the same. There are 5 niches in the kiva wall.

The masonry of this kiva is fairly good, its western wall naturally being the most destroyed. The banquette over the tunnel into kiva A is broader than any of the others. On the eastern side the kiva walls are apparently double.

---

[50] The measurements of the kivas here given were determined by Mr. R. G. Fuller, who served as voluntary assistant during the summer.

[51] With the exception of that in kiva Q there has not been found in any deflector a large stone ("fire stone") forming the cap or top. In deflectors formed of a slab of stone such a "fire stone" on top would be impossible.

PLATE 23

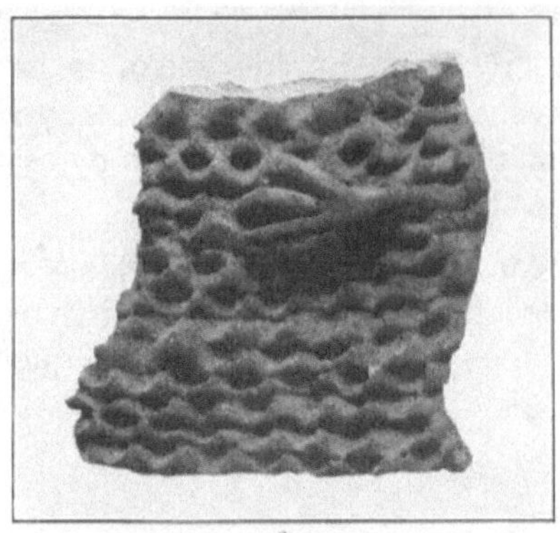

VARIOUS OBJECTS FROM CLIFF PALACE

*a. Pottery fragment with bird-claw decoration in relief , b, d. Food bowls, c. Incised stone,
e. Decorated fragment of earthenware , f. Cover for vase*

Kiva C

This kiva is circular; it measures 13 feet in diameter, and 5 feet 6 inches from the floor to the top of the pilasters. The height of the banquette is 3 feet. The number of pilasters is 6; their average breadth is 2 feet.

The deflector is a stone wall laid in mortar; its width is 3 feet 6 inches; the thickness, 8 inches. From the flue to the deflector is 2 feet 4 inches, and from the same to the fire-hole, 8 inches. The diameter of the fire-hole is 2 feet, its depth 1 foot. The sipapû is 2 feet from the fire-hole; it is 6 inches deep and 4 inches in diameter.

The masonry of this kiva was in very poor condition, most of the upper part being wholly broken down. There are 4 niches in the walls. The surface is thickly plastered and shows a deposit of smoke. The pilasters are of uniform size. The deep banquette is situated above the flue back of the deflector.

Kiva D

Kiva D is square, with rounded corners; it is 13 feet in diameter; its walls are 10 feet high and measure 7 feet from the floor to the top of the pilasters. The height of the banquette is 4 feet. The number of pilasters is 6; their average distance apart is 4 feet 6 inches, and their width 2 feet. The eastern wall of this kiva is the side of the cave, and the whole was inclosed by high walls. On the southern side of the kiva is a passageway. The walls of the kiva and the cave roof above it are blackened with smoke. There are two deep banquettes.

The flue opens in the western wall of the kiva; its height is 2 feet, and its width at the top is 13 inches. The distance from the flue to the deflector is 2 feet 6 inches; from the deflector to the fire-hole, 13 inches. The diameter of the fire-hole is 2 feet and its depth 1 foot. The distance from the fire-hole to the sipapû is 2 feet 2 inches; the diameter of the latter is 3 inches. This kiva has 5 finely made rectangular niches in the walls. The walls are well plastered and were painted yellow. Wherever the masonry is visible it is found inferior to none except possibly that of kiva Q.[52]

Kiva E

Kiva E is square, with rounded corners; it measures 11 feet 6 inches in diameter, and is 9 feet 10 inches high. The elevation of the banquette is 4 feet, and of the pilasters 7 feet. The number of pilasters is 6. The flue opens on the western side.

The deflector consists of a wall of stone, 2 feet high; its width is 3 feet 6 inches, the thickness 9 inches. The distance from the deflector to the flue is 1 foot 10 inches, and from the fire-hole 3 inches. There are 4 mural niches. As the projecting rock on the eastern side interfered with the symmetry of this kiva, when constructed it was necessary to peck the rock away 8 inches deep over an area 10 feet square, thus exhibiting, next to the floor of kiva V, the most extensive piece of kiva stone-cutting in Cliff Palace. Although this kiva was generally in a fair state of preservation, it was necessary to rebuild much of the eastern wall.

---

[52] This kiva, which is one of the best in Cliff Palace, is illustrated by Nordenskiöld.

The fire-hole of this kiva is lined with a rude jar set with adobe mortar. No sipapû was discovered in the floor. Kiva E is one of the few kivas in Cliff Palace surrounded by the walls of rooms. As it is situated in the rear of the cave, projecting walls of the cliff were necessarily cut away to a considerable extent in order to obtain the form of room desired on the eastern side. This side of the kiva is blackened by smoke antedating the construction of the room. There is abundant evidence in this portion of the ruin of secondary construction of buildings on the same site. Several walls built upon others show that some rooms may have been abandoned and new ones added, an indication that this portion of the ruin is very old, perhaps having the oldest walls still standing.

Kiva F

Kiva F, situated on a lower terrace than the kivas already described, is square, with rounded corners, and is 9 feet high. The height of the pilasters is 6 feet 10 inches, and the top of the banquette is 4 feet 1 inch above the floor. The diameter of the kiva is 13 feet. There are 6 pilasters; the distance between them averages 5 feet; their average width is 2 feet 4 inches. The deflector, a wall of masonry, is 3 feet wide and averages 9 inches in thickness.

The deflector is 2 feet from the flue and 18 inches from the fire-hole, which is 2 feet in diameter and the same in depth. The distance from the fire-hole to the sipapû is 2 feet 4 inches. The diameter of the sipapû is 2½ inches, and its depth 5 inches.

There are 3 mural niches, similar to those previously described. The roof of this kiva was of the same level as the floors of rooms 16 and 24, the roofs of which overlooked the kiva situated in the terrace below.

The walls of this kiva are black with smoke. The room is surrounded by a second wall, the interval between which and that of the kiva is filled with rubble.

Kiva G

This kiva may be called "heartshaped." Its height from the floor to the top of the roof is 9 feet, and it measures 6 feet from the floor to the top of the pilasters. The banquette is 4 feet high, and the interior diameter of the kiva is 12 feet. The numbers of pilasters is 6; their average breadth is a little more than 2 feet, and the intervals between them averages 3 feet 6 inches.

The deflector is a stone slab 3 feet wide and 2 feet high. The distance from the flue to the deflector is 2 feet; from the deflector to the fire-hole 11 inches. The diameter of the fire-hole is 2 feet, its depth 18 inches. The sipapû is 2 feet 8 inches from the fire-hole; its diameter is 2 inches, and its depth 4 inches. There are 4 mural niches.

This kiva is situated in the terrace below that last mentioned, that is, in the second terrace, and was wholly buried when excavations began. The roofs of rooms 30 and 31 overlooked this kiva, their floors being on the same level as the kiva roof.

PLATE 24

FOOD BOWLS

Kiva H

Kiva H (pl. 18) measures 8 feet from the floor to the top of the wall, and 6 feet from the floor to the top of the pilasters. The height of the banquette is 4 feet 6 inches. The diameter of the kiva is 11 feet 6 inches.

The deflector is a curved stone wall joining the kiva wall on each side of the flue.[53] It is built of stone, 7 feet 6 inches high, 10 inches wide, and 20 inches high. The deflector is 1 foot 6 inches from the flue and 15 inches from the fire-hole. The diameter of the fire-hole is 2 feet and its depth 1 foot.

The sipapû is situated 2 feet from the fire-hole; it is 3 inches in diameter and 4 inches deep.

There are 2 mural niches. Exceptional features of this kiva are the curved deflector and the opening into a small room at the northwestern corner. Instead of extending straight from the kiva to the vertical ventilator, the flue turns at a right angle midway in its course. The ventilator is built at one corner of the kiva wall. As this kiva lies deep below the base of the round tower, a fine view of these several characteristics may be obtained from that point.

---

[53] A similar deflector is recorded by Mr. Morley as existing in the Cannonball ruin, and is figured by Nordenskiöld from the Mesa Verde.

Kiva I

When work began there was no indication of the walls of this kiva, except a fragment of one which at first was supposed to belong to a small secular room. The kiva had been filled with débris by those who had dug into the upper rooms, and a large hole[54] was broken through the high western wall of kiva L, through which to throw débris. The removal of this accumulation was a work of considerable magnitude, and the repair of the kiva wall was very difficult, as it was necessary to reconstruct the foundations that had been blasted away to make the opening above mentioned.

When this débris was removed and the floor of the kiva was reached, it was found that its walls were much disintegrated, the component stones having practically turned into sand, necessitating the construction of buttresses to support them. The dimensions of kiva I are as follows: The height of the top of the wall from the floor is 8 feet, and that of the pilasters 6 feet 8 inches. The banquette rises 3 feet 8 inches above the floor. The interior diameter of the kiva is 10 feet 10 inches. The number of pedestals is 4, averaging 4 feet in height.

The flue is situated at the southwestern side. The distance from the flue to the deflector is 21 inches; from the deflector to the fire-hole, 2 inches. There are two mural niches, one at the northeast measuring 13 by 11 by 8 inches, and one at the southeast measuring 13 by 11 by 7 inches. A dado, painted red, surrounded the kiva, the color being most conspicuous, because best protected, in the mural niches, half of which are above, half below the upper margin of the dado. On this margin are traceable triangular figures like those on the painted wall of room 11.

On the level of what was formerly the roof of this kiva was set into the roof a vase covered with a flat stone and containing desiccated bodies of lizards.[55]

Kiva J

Kiva J is round; it is 14 feet in diameter and measures 8 feet 4 inches from the floor to the top of the wall. The height from the floor to the top of one of the pilasters is 5 feet 10 inches. The banquette is 3 feet 2 inches high. The deep banquette, as is usually the case, is above the flue, which opens in the southwestern wall. The number of pedestals is 6; their average breadth is 2 feet. The deflector consists of a stone wall rising 20 inches above the kiva floor. There are 7 mural niches. The kiva walls were thickly plastered with adobe, and show the action of smoke.[56]

The open space east of the kiva, formerly continuous with its roof, is somewhat larger than is usually the case, making this the largest plaza in Cliff Palace, except that of the plaza quarter. There are remnants of rooms southwest of the kiva.

---

[54] This entrance in the wall appears in all photographs of this portion of Cliff Palace.

[55] For a note on a similar vase and its use, see remarks on kiva S. It is probable that these dried lizards were regarded by the Cliff Palace priests as very potent "medicine."

[56] From all appearances the kivas were plastered from time to time after the walls had become blackened.

PLATE 25

a   b

c   d

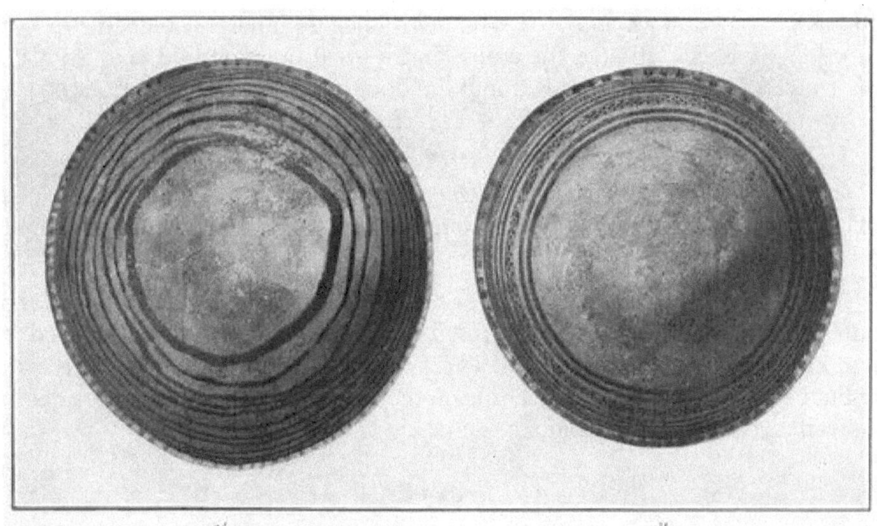

c'   d'

VASES AND FOOD BOWLS

Kiva K

Kiva K[57] is round in form, and its height from the floor to the roof is 7 feet. The height of the pilasters is 5 feet, and that of the banquette 3 feet. The diameter of the kiva is 9 feet 6 inches. The pilasters are 5 in number, and average about 20 inches in width. The deflector of this kiva is exceptional, being the only known instance where this structure is constructed of upright stakes bound with twigs or cedar bark and plastered with adobe.[58] The distance from the flue to the deflector is 18 inches, and from the deflector to the fire-hole, 8 inches. The diameter of the fire-hole is 20 inches, the depth 8 inches. The walls of this smallest of the kivas are formed partly of masonry, but in places the chamber is excavated out of solid rock, the ancient builders having pecked away projections in order to produce the desired form.

The marks of smoke are clearly visible, especially on the flue; and on the surface of the eastern side are scratched several figures representing birds and other animals. Eyelets of osiers set in the wall are also exceptional, and their use is problematical.

Kiva L

The height of kiva L is 7 feet 5 inches, that of the pilasters 5 feet 4 inches, and of the banquette 3 feet 3 inches. The diameter is 12 feet 2 inches. Number of pilasters 6. The flue opens on the western side; its height is 2 feet. Only a single mural niche was recognizable.

The walls of this kiva were very badly damaged, the whole of its front having fallen inward, covering the floor. The construction of the room demanded considerable rock cutting, especially on the eastern side, to secure the requisite depth. Whatever masonry remained in position was, as a rule, good. Probably no kiva in Cliff Palace was more dilapidated when work began. It had been used as a dump by those who had mutilated the ruins, and a great opening had been torn in its western wall. Excavations showed that the floor had been wholly destroyed.

Kiva N

The height of kiva N is 7 feet 4 inches, and that of the pilasters 5 feet 4 inches. The banquette is 3 feet high. The diameter of the kiva is 11 feet. There are 6 pilasters and 5 mural niches.

This kiva was in bad condition when the work began, but it is now in good repair and exhibits interesting features. The deflector was wholly destroyed, and it was impossible to find the sipapû. There are evidences of considerable rock cutting on the northern side, and of a little on the eastern and southwestern sides. The kiva walls are blackened by smoke.

Kiva P

------

[57] This kiva, one of the finest and in some features the most exceptional in Cliff Palace, is not indicated in Nordenskiöld's plan.

[58] Nordenskiöld describes a ventilator constructed in the same way.

The height of kiva P is 8 feet, its diameter 11 feet 3 inches. The height from the floor to the top of a pilaster is 5 feet 10 inches, and to the top of the banquette 3 feet 4 inches. The number of pilasters is 6, and their average breadth about 20 inches.

From the flue to the deflector the distance is 2 feet 8 inches, and the deflector is situated 6 inches from the fire-hole. There are 5 mural niches.

The walls of this kiva are much blackened by smoke. The masonry is fair, but much broken on the northern and western sides. There is evidence that a considerable amount of rock has been pecked away on the northern side to the floor level. The kiva occupies almost the whole open space in which it is constructed, and the walls of neighboring buildings surround it on all sides, rising from the edge of the kiva. In order to secure a level foundation, parallel beams to support the floor were laid from a projecting rock to a masonry wall. The ends of these logs project above the path that leads to the main entrance.

Kiva Q

This kiva (pl. 19) is round in shape and measures 8 feet 6 inches from the floor to the top of the wall. There were formerly eight pilasters, which averaged 18 inches in breadth. The height of the pilasters is 6 feet, and of the top of the banquette 3 feet 3 inches. The diameter of the kiva is 13 feet 8 inches.

The fire-hole is 22 inches from the deflector; the thickness of the latter is 10 inches, and its width 3 feet 3 inches. There are four mural niches, all in fine condition. Although the masonry of this kiva is the finest in Cliff Palace, its whole western end is destroyed. The floor west of the deflector has a slightly convex surface.[59]

No ceremonial opening, or sipapû, such as occurs in several other Cliff Palace kivas, was found in kiva Q. At the place where this feature usually appears the floor was broken, but as several of the Cliff Palace kivas have no specialized sipapûs it is possible that this device may be looked for in another opening in the floor. There are no sipapûs in the Hano kivas of the East Mesa of the Hopi, and the priests of that pueblo assert that the Tewa have no special hole in the kiva floor to represent this ceremonial opening. Apparently the Pueblos of the Rio Grande are like the Tewa of Hano in this respect. All the kivas of Spruce-tree House and a number of those in Cliff Palace have this ceremonial opening, thus following the Hopi rather than the Tewa custom. Whether the fireplace was used by those who performed rites in kiva Q as a symbolic opening into or from the "underworld" is unknown, to the writer. The subterranean passage in kiva V leading to the fire-hole, but not entering it, is interesting in this particular. Kiva V, however, as pointed out, has in addition to the fire-hole a fine pottery-lined sipapû corresponding to the sipapûs in Hopi kivas, but made in the solid rock floor.

---

[59] In ceremonial rooms of ruins in the Navaho National Monument this curve is represented by a raised step.

PLATE 26

a Mugs from crematory

b Dipper-bowl and corrugated vase

POTTERY

Kiva S

This kiva is square, with rounded corners. Its height is 8 feet, and the height of one of the pilasters above the floor 5 feet 10 inches. The banquettes are 3 feet 3 inches above the floor. The diameter of the kiva is 10 feet 4 inches.

The number of pilasters is 6; their average breadth is 20 inches. The distance from flue to deflector, which is a slab of stone, is 3 feet 2 inches; the height of the deflector is 1 foot 7 inches and its width 3 feet.

From the deflector to the fire-hole the distance is 7 inches. The diameter of the fire-hole is 2 feet, its depth 9 inches. There are 2 mural niches. The large banquette is 3 feet 6 inches broad. The shaft of the flue, after passing 18 inches under the kiva wall, turns southeastward 4 feet 4 inches and then takes a vertical course. The masonry of kiva S is fairly good. A jar is set into one of the banquettes, and was perhaps formerly used for containing sacred meal.[60] This receptacle was left as found, and a slab of stone placed slantingly above it to shield it from falling stones. Under the huge rock above it there are light masonry walls outlining diminutive rooms used possibly for storage but not for habitation.

Kiva T

This kiva stands on an elevated rock, and has double walls, the intervals between the wall of the kiva and the outside walls being filled with rubble.

The height of kiva T is 7 feet 6 inches, that of one of the pilasters 6 feet 6 inches. The banquette is 3 feet 9 inches above the floor. The diameter of the kiva is 10 feet 5 inches. There were probably 6 pilasters and 2 mural niches. Although the greater part of the walls of this kiva was destroyed, a deep banquette still remains above the air shaft. The floor has the same level as the second terrace, or one story above kiva S, the roof of which is consequently at the level of the floor of kiva T.

Kiva T was in bad condition when work began, as part of its front wall had fallen and only the tops of the others were visible above the débris. Even the floor level was difficult to determine.

Kiva U

The form of kiva U is round, and its height is 7 feet 6 inches. The height of one of the pilasters is 4 feet 11 inches, and that of the banquette 3 feet 4 inches. The diameter of the kiva is 12 feet. There are 5 pilasters. The fire-hole is 4 inches from the flue; the diameter of the fire-hole is 20 inches, its depth 6 inches. There are 6 mural niches, so arranged that two large niches are situated above two small ones. The presence of but 5 pedestals is accounted for by the joining of 2 above the flue. Much rock-cutting was necessary in constructing this kiva, especially on the northern and southwestern sides. As the front wall of the kiva had fallen, it had to be practically rebuilt. The foundations were unstable, apparently having been constructed on loose stones carelessly laid.

Kiva V

This kiva is round and measures 5 feet 6 inches from the floor to the top of one

---

[60] Among the Hopi at the present day certain fetishes, as the effigies of the Great Plumed Serpent, are regarded as so sacred that when not in use they are kept in jars set in a banquette, the surface of which is level with the neck of the jar. These receptacles are closely sealed with a stone slab when the images are deposited in them. Possibly the jars set in the kiva banquettes of Cliff Palace may have been used for a similar purpose: i. e., were receptacles for fetishes held in such veneration that, as is the case with the Great Serpent effigies of the Hopi, one even touching them may, in the belief of the people, be afflicted with direful disorders.

of the pilasters. The top of the banquette is 3 feet 4 inches above the floor. The diameter of the kiva is 12 feet 8 inches. The number of pilasters is 6 and their average breadth 20 inches.

The distance from the deflector to the line of the wall is 23 inches; the height, of the deflector is 22 inches, the thickness 9 inches, and the width 3 feet 2 inches. The fire-hole is 18 inches from the sipapû; the latter is 10 inches deep and 3 inches in diameter, and is lined with a pottery tube cemented in place. There are three mural niches.

Kiva V is exceptional in the amount of rock-cutting that was necessary for lowering the floor to the desired level. Probably the greatest amount of stone-cutting was done in this kiva.

There remains to be mentioned a unique tunnel which may eventually throw some light on ceremonial openings in the kivas of cliff-dwellings. Just beneath the adobe floor, extending from a vertical flue outside the kiva to the fire-hole, which it does not, however, enter, there is a passage through which a small person may crawl. Exteriorly this opens into a vertical flue which was broken down; inside it ends bluntly at the fire-hole. About midway of its length there extends from it a lateral passageway, slightly curved, forming a well-worn doorway. This curved passage opens through the kiva floor by a manhole. The walls of these passages are constructed of good masonry. Their function is unknown, but as most structures connected with kivas are ceremonial, this may provisionally be called a ceremonial opening.

It is evident that this ceremonial passage had nothing to do or at least had no connection with the ventilator and deflector of the kiva. The opening is situated under the floor, passing in its course beneath the deflector, and its external opening is by a vertical passage outside the ventilator. It also differs from the ventilator in having a lateral branch likewise situated under the floor. Passing to kivas outside the Mesa Verde region, we find homologous passages recorded as present under the floor in Pueblo Bonito, a ruin on the Chaco, and in the kiva of a ruin not far from Chama, where the passage under the floor is excavated in solid rock. Evidently we have in this structure a ceremonial opening the true significance of which is yet to be determined. Is it connected with the Tewa concept that the fire-hole is a sipapû, or was it used in fire rites that were performed about the fireplace? These and other questions that might be proposed must remain unanswered until more is known of similar passages in other cliff-dwelling kivas.

PLATE 27

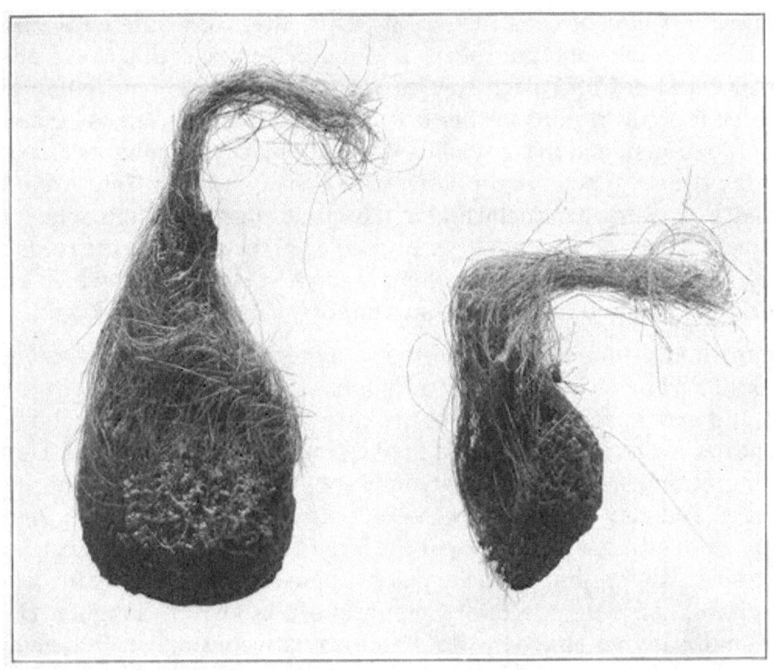

PITCH BALLS AND VASE

A SUBTYPE OF KIVA (KIVA M)

The method of roof construction, which is the main difference that distinguishes a kiva of the subtype from one of the first type, is due to the absence of pilasters. Kiva M of Cliff Palace may be assigned to this subtype, although many examples of it occur in ruins farther down the San Juan, as well as in the Navaho National Monument and in Canyon de Chelly. Kivas of the subtype are similar to those of the second type in that pilasters are absent, but they differ from them in the presence of a large banquette and in the subterranean position, which features also characterize the first type. The only circular kivas known to the ruins near the East Mesa of the Hopi of Arizona belong to the first type, two of which are found at Kukuchomo, the two ruins on the summit of the mesa above Sikyatki.

The method of roofing a kiva of the subtype may be clearly observed in the kiva of Scaffold House in the Navaho National Monument.[61] The rafters here are parallel, and extend across the top of the kiva, their ends resting on the wall. The middle beam, which is the largest, is flanked on each side by another. Upon these supporting beams are laid others at right angles, and on these were placed the brush, bark, and clay that covered the roof. Entrance was gained by means of a hatchway on one side of the roof near the large banquette, which occupies a position, as respects the entrance and the place supposedly occupied by the ladder and the fire-pit, similar to the spectator's platform of a modern rectangular Hopi kiva, except that it is higher above the floor and is relatively smaller. If the banquettes were depressed and enlarged into a platform, the form of the kiva being changed from circular to rectangular, thus modified the banquette would form a structure like the spectator's platform of a typical modern Hopi kiva.[62]

Perhaps of all the ceremonial rooms repaired the walls of kiva M were in the most dangerous condition. The front of the northern wall of room 39 had been undermined and was without foundation, hanging without basal support except at the ends. A support was constructed under this hanging wall, and to give additional strength the foundations were rebuilt a little broader at the base than formerly, causing the wall to bulge almost imperceptibly into the kiva. Although no pilasters were seen, the deep banquette on the northwestern side places it among the kivas of the first type.

KIVAS OF THE SECOND TYPE

The architecture of the two kivas O and R are so different from those already considered that they are set apart from the others in a second type. The form and structure of kiva W indicate that this room also may be classed as of the same type. In the side canyon north of that in which Cliff Palace is situated, where water was obtained throughout the summer, there is another kiva, also supposed to belong to the second type.[63]

---

[61] See *Bulletin 50, Bureau of American Ethnology.*

[62] The two circular kivas of Kukuchomo, near Sikyatki, have this large banquette and in other respects resemble the ruins of Canyon de Chelly. Kukuchomo marks the site of a settlement, of the Coyote clan of the Hopi in prehistoric times.

[63] As a huge rock had fallen from the roof of the cave in which this kiva lies, since it

The main difference in construction between the two types of kivas is the absence of pilasters, which implies the absence of a roof in the second type. The suggestion that a kiva of the second type is simply an unfinished form of the first type has little to support it, but whether the architectural difference in the two types has any functional importance or meaning is unknown. It has been suggested that one type was used by the Winter, the other by the Summer people.[64]

PLATE 28

RESTS FOR JARS

Kiva O

Kiva O is rounded below and square above, with a north-south diameter of 11 feet 10 inches, and an east-west diameter of 10 feet 6 inches. The ventilator opens in the western wall. There are 2 mural niches.

Both the plastered floor and the deflector are lacking, and there is no fire-hole nor sipapû. No roof or pilasters to support it were detected. It is difficult to measure the surrounding wall on account of its varying height. The masonry is good, but there are no signs on the walls that a fire had ever burned within the chamber. It would appear that this kiva was roofless, and that it had broad banquettes at the northern and southern sides.

Kiva R

In shape this kiva is oval below and square above, without pilasters or other evidences of a roof. There are no signs of a floor, a deflector, or a fire-hole. The surrounding wall of the kiva is high; apparently there was an entrance at the eastern side. Banquettes are present on the northern and southern ends, and a narrow ledge skirts the other two sides.

---

was first occupied, it would appear that the place was abandoned on that account.

[64] Nordenskiöld's description of this kiva has been quoted earlier in this paper. In the description of a ceremonial room of a somewhat similar or of the same type in Spruce-tree House the term "warrior room" is used; there is nothing to warrant this designation, however, and it would be better to consider it simply as a kiva of the second type.

There are 4 mural niches: (1) south by east, measuring 15 by 11 by 13 inches; (1) north by east, measuring 11½ by 8 by 15 inches; (2) in the north wall, measuring 13 by 8 by 12 inches, and 12 by 8 by 13 inches; the latter three being placed in a row and separated by slabs of stone. In the south wall there is a tunnel terminating bluntly and bifurcated at the end.

Although kiva R was regarded by Nordenskiöld as furnishing evidence of a transition form connecting circular and rectangular kivas, it seems to the author a new type rather than a modification of the circular or the rectangular kivas.

Kiva W

Kiva W is not generally included among the Cliff Palace ceremonial rooms on account of its isolation from the houses, but there is no doubt that it should be so enumerated. It lies about 50 feet west of the end of the last room in the cliff-dwelling, and is not accompanied with secular rooms. Although situated on the same level as the houses, its walls rise two tiers high, but no part of the inclosure is subterranean.

From the height of the walls it at first seemed as if in kiva W there were evidences of a room above. This condition would be contrary to the rule and, to the Hopi mind, ceremonially impossible; but if its upper walls are regarded as homogeneous with the high walls that surround kivas O and R, and we interpret this as an example of the second type of kiva, the anomaly is explained.

Although this kiva is placed provisionally in the second type mainly because of these lofty side walls, on account of its isolation at the end of Cliff Palace several observers have not regarded it as belonging to the ruin. Neither Nordenskiöld nor Morley and Kidder included it in their ground plans, nor does Nordenskiöld mention it in his enumeration of Cliff Palace kivas.

As kiva W is almost wholly unprotected by the cave roof, its walls have greatly suffered from the downpour of rains to which they are exposed. The masonry is fairly good. Evidently it was an important building, and was isolated from other rooms possibly for some special purpose. As there are few or no walls of secular rooms near it, one may believe that it was resorted to by the villagers on special occasions and did not belong to any one clan.

MINOR ANTIQUITIES

In the preceding pages have been described the major antiquities, such as walls and those permanent objects which could not be removed from the places where they were constructed without more or less harm. There remain to be considered the minor antiquities, or the smaller objects which are movable and of a more perishable nature, especially if left in the places where they were found. It was mainly in search of such objects that much of the mutilation of Cliff Palace was done.

It was not expected that excavations would yield any considerable number of specimens, since for years Cliff Palace had been dug over in search of them, and many hundreds of objects had already been found and carried away to be sold either to museums or to individuals. Notwithstanding these unfavorable conditions, the collection of objects, now deposited in the National Museum, is sufficient to afford some idea of the culture of the Cliff Palace people.

Among the objects that may be mentioned in the category of minor antiquities are pottery, basketry, implements of stone, bone, and wood, fabrics of various kinds, ornaments, fetishes, and the like—all those objects commonly called artifacts that make up collections from cliff-dwellings generally.

The excavations at Cliff Palace have revealed no specimens strikingly different from those already described as from Spruce-tree House. We would expect some variation in the symbols on pottery from the two ruins, but the differences are not conspicuous in the few specimens that have been compared. Nor is there any peculiarity in the form of the pottery, as the ceramic objects from Cliff Palace practically duplicate those from Spruce-tree House, already described, and probably are not much unlike those still buried in Long House, Balcony House, and the House with the Square Tower.

As many ceremonial objects, being highly prized, may have been removed from Cliff Palace when the place was deserted by its inhabitants, the few that remained present scant material from which to add to our knowledge of the ceremonial life of the people. The existence of so many kivas would point to many rites, although a large number of sacred rooms does not necessarily indicate more complex or elaborate rites than a smaller number: multiplicity of kivas does not necessarily mean multiplicity of ceremonies, nor few kivas a limited ritual. In no pueblo are there more complicated ceremonies than at Walpi, where there are only five of these sacred rooms; but it must be remembered that many of the religious rites of Walpi are performed in kihus, or secular rooms. The same may have been true of Cliff Palace.

PLATE 29

BASKET HOPPER—SIDE AND BOTTOM VIEWS

The writer's belief is that in historic times, by which is meant since the advent of missionaries, altars have become more elaborate and rites more complex at Walpi than in prehistoric times, and that through the same influence the use of images or idols has also increased. This increase in the complexity of rites may be traced to the amalgamation of clans or to a substitution of the fraternities of priesthoods for simple clan ancestor worship. The elaborate character of ceremonial paraphernalia may likewise be due to acculturation,[65] which increases in complication with the lapse of time.

STONE IMPLEMENTS

The stone implements from Cliff Palace consist of axes, mauls, paint grinders, pecking stones, metates, balls, flakes, spear and arrow points, and various other articles (pls. 20-22). There is great uniformity in these implements, the axes, for instance, being generally single edged, although a good specimen of double-edged hatchet is in the collection. A fragment of the peculiar stone implement called *tcamahia*[66] by the Hopi was found.

While as a rule the hatchets are without handles, one specimen (pl. 20) is exceptional in this particular. The handle of this hatchet from Cliff Palace, like that from Spruce-tree House, elsewhere described, is a stick bent in a loop around the stone head.

Pounding Stones

Anyone who will examine the amount of stone-cutting necessary to lower the floor of kiva V, for instance, to its present depth, or to peck away the projecting rock in some of the other kivas, will realize at once that the Cliff Palace people were industrious stone workers. A number of the pounding stones (pl. 22, *a*) with which this work was done have been found. These stones are cubical in form, or rounded or pointed at one end or both ends, and provided with two or more pits on the sides. They were evidently held directly in the hand and used without handles. Although generally small, they sometimes are of considerable size. The stone of which they are made is foreign to the vicinity; it is hard, as would be absolutely necessary to be effectual in the use to which they were put.

Grinding Stones

The most common variety of grinding stones is, of course, the metate, or millstone, used in grinding corn. These implements have a variety of forms. They may be flat above and rounded below, or flat on both sides, triangular on each face, or simply convex on each side. None of them have feet like the Mexican metates. The

---

[65] For instance, the complicated reredos of many of the modern Hopi altars is made of flat wooden slabs, the manufacture of which would be very difficult for a people ignorant of iron. These probably replaced painted stone slabs of simpler character, examples of which have been found in ruins and indeed still survive in some of the oldest rites.

[66] This object probably came from near Tokónabi, the ancient home of the Snake people of Walpi, on San Juan river. Fourteen of these tcamahias form part of the Antelope altar in the Snake Dance at Walpi.

stone with which the grinding was done, or the one held in the hand, also varies in shape, size, and evidences of use.[67] Stones with a depression in one face served as mortars. A stone in the form of a pestle, flat on the end, served as a paint grinder. Several flat stones with smooth surface, showing the effect of grinding, and others with slight concavities, undoubtedly served the same purpose. Smooth stones showing grinding on one or more faces were evidently the implements with which the builders smoothed the walls of the houses after the masonry had been laid; others were used in polishing pottery.

PLATE 30

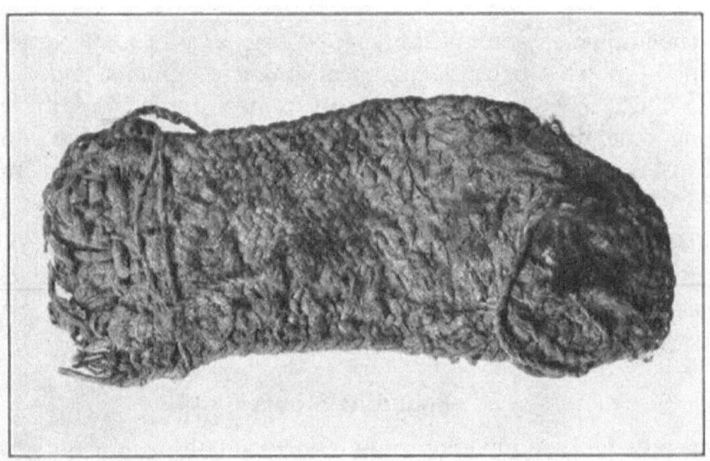

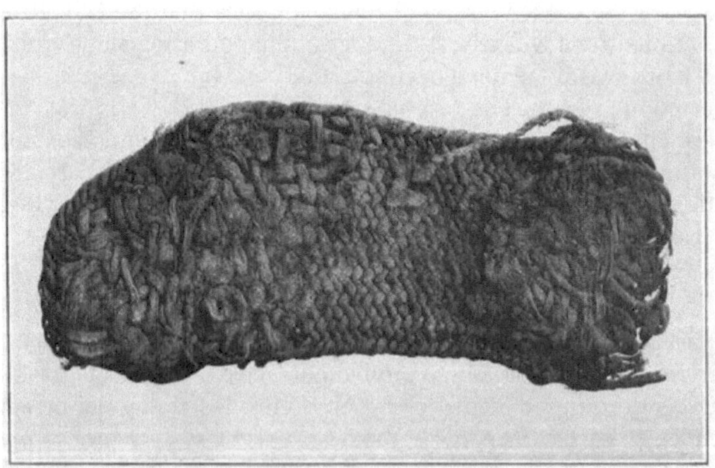

SANDALS

[67] At several places on the surfaces of projecting rocks forming the foundations of buildings may be noticed grooves where metates were sharpened. One or more of these occur at the entrance to the "street" in front of room 51. The foundation of a wall in one room was built directly upon one of these grooves, part of the groove being in sight, the rest covered with masonry. Near room 92 there are many of these grooves as well as small pits.

PLATE 31

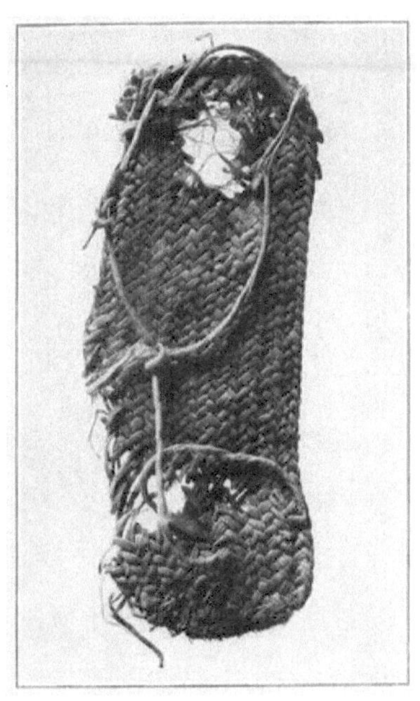 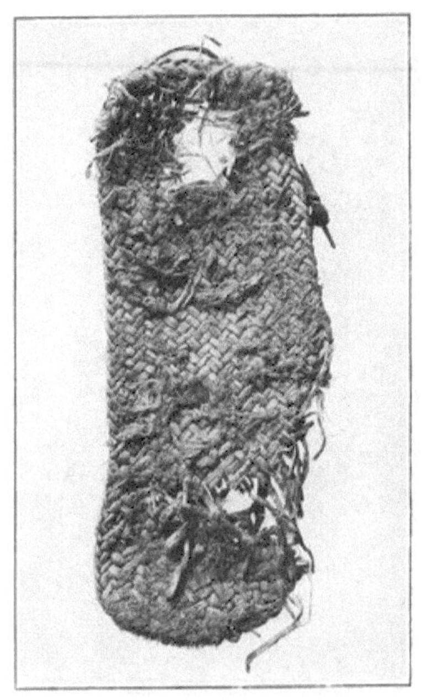

SANDALS

PLATE 32

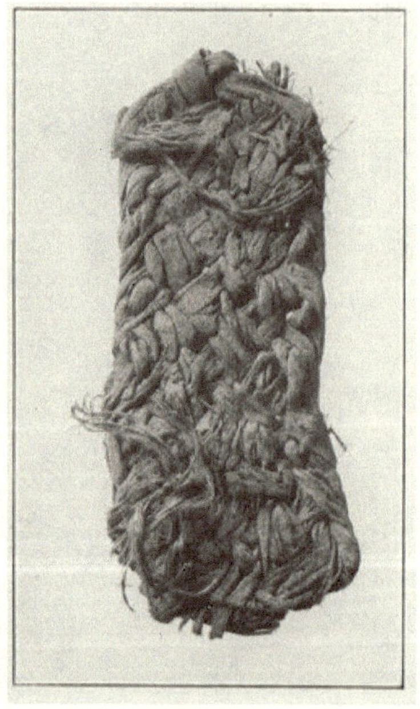

SANDALS

Miscellaneous Stones

Many stone balls, large or small, were found. Some of these show chipping, others are ground smooth. Certain of these balls were evidently used in a game popular at Cliff Palace, in which they were rolled or dropped into deep pits and grooves. It appears that this game was played by occupants of the sacred rooms, as the pits are common in the kiva floors. Other stone balls were formerly tied to the end of a handle with a thong of hide and used as a weapon.

A half oval stone, smooth and flat at one pole, is supposed to have been an idol, possibly the earth goddess, who is repeatedly represented by the Hopi in a similar way. It was left near where it was found at the northwest corner of kiva H. Our masons used rectangular slabs of soft stone, which were doubtless door-closes, as mortar boards. They were held in place in the door opening by jambs made of mortar laid on sticks, and by a horizontal rod which passed between two osier eyelets set in the uprights of the door-frame and projecting from it. These stone doors were sometimes held in place by a groove cut in the threshold or by a ledge of adobe.

Two thin, flat, circular stone disks (pl. 22, *c*), with smooth surfaces and square edges, accompanied the calcined human bones in the inclosure at the northern end of the large refuse heap. It is probable that some of these disks were used as covers for mortuary vases. Irregularly shaped flat stones with pits and incised figures pecked in their surface were used in a game, and a slab covered with incised figures but without the pits (pl. 23, *c*) probably served a similar purpose.

Several large stones, which the builders of Cliff Palace had begun to dress and had later rejected, show the method adopted by them in cutting stones the required size. When stones were found to be too large to be laid, or had projections that interfered with the required shape, a groove was pecked where the fracture was desired and the stone broken along the groove.

POTTERY

No ruin in the Mesa Verde National Park has yielded more specimens of pottery than Cliff Palace, many pieces of which are preserved in various museums in Colorado and elsewhere. The collection gathered by the writer was small compared with some of these, and although only a few whole pieces were found, by restoration from fragments a fair number of specimens, ample perhaps for generalization, were procured. In the following mention of the pottery obtained from the ruin a very comprehensive idea of the perfection in the ceramic art attained in Cliff Palace can hardly be hoped.

Southwestern pottery may be divided into two types, so far as superficial appearance goes: (1) coiled or indented undecorated ware; (2) smooth polished ware. Of the latter there are two sub-types: (*a*) pottery with a surface slip, generally white, on which designs are painted, and (*b*) decorated pottery without a superficial slip, and generally reddish in color. Cliff Palace pottery, when decorated, belongs to the last two divisions, but some of the best made specimens belong to the coiled or indented type. Although there are several fragments of red pottery ornamented with designs painted in black, and one or two specimens in which the basal color is orange, the majority of the specimens belong to the so-called black-and-white ware, which may therefore be called a type of this region.

The whole pieces of pottery collected were chiefly mortuary vessels, and probably contained food offerings, indicating, like the sipapûs in the kivas, that the cliff-dwellers had a distinct conception of a future life. In addition to the limited number of pieces of unbroken pottery, many of the fragments were decorated with novel patterns. Fragments of corrugated and indented ware are by far the most numerous, but although many of these were obtained, not a whole piece was found, with the exception of a single specimen plastered in a fire-hole and three others similarly fixed in the banquettes of kivas. These were left as they were found.

The same forms of pottery, as dippers, ladles, vases, canteens, jars, and similar objects, occur at Cliff Palace as at Spruce-tree House (pl. 23-27). All varieties were repeatedly found, some with old cracks that had been mended, and one is still tied with the yucca cord with which it had been repaired. It is evident from the frequency with which the Cliff Palace people mended their old pottery that they prized the old vessels and were very careful to preserve them, being loth to abandon even a cracked jar (pl. 23, *d*). None of the Cliff Palace pottery is glazed.[68] Some specimens of smooth pottery are coarse in texture and without decoration; others have elaborate geometrical figures; but animate objects are confined almost entirely to a few pictures of birds or other animals and rudely drawn human figures. The pictography of the pottery affords scant data bearing on the interpretation of the ancient symbolism of the inhabitants, as compared with that of Sikyatki, for example, in the Hopi country.

Food bowls.—In form the food bowls[69] from Cliff Palace (pls. 23-25) are the same as those from other prehistoric sites of the Southwest, but as a rule the Cliff Palace bowls are smaller than those of Sikyatki and the ruins on the Little Colorado. They have, as a rule, a thicker lip, which is square across instead of tapering to a thin edge or flaring, as is sometimes the case elsewhere. The surface, inside and out, is commonly very smooth, even glossy. The pottery was built up by coiling the clay, and the colors were made permanent by the firing.

The basis of the study of symbolism was of course the pottery decoration. As a rule the center of the inside of the food bowls is plain, but several have this portion ornamented with squares, triangles, and other figures. The outside of several bowls from Cliff Palace and Spruce-tree House is decorated, notwithstanding Nordenskiöld speaks of exterior decoration as rare in his collections from the Mesa Verde. The geometric ornaments consist of rectangular figures.[70]

[68] The first description of "glazed" pottery in the Pueblo region is given by Castañeda (1540), who says: "Throughout this province [Tiguex] are found glazed pottery and vessels truly remarkable both in shape and execution." This has sometimes been interpreted to mean the glossy but unglazed pottery of Santa Clara. Glazed pottery was found by the writer in 1896 in ruins on the Little Colorado. It appears to be intrusive in the Arizona ruins.

[69] Food bowls with handles, so common to the ruins of northern Arizona, were not found at Cliff Palace.

[70] No curved lines are present in the many examples of decoration on the outside of food bowls from Sikyatki.

Mugs.—Some authors have questioned whether the prehistoric people of the Southwest were familiar with this form of pottery. The collections from Cliff Palace (pl. 24-26) and Spruce-tree House set at rest any reasonable doubt on this point. There are, however, peculiarities in the form of mugs from Mesa Verde. The diameter of the base is generally larger, tapering gently toward the mouth, and one end of the handle is rarely affixed to the rim. The inside of the mug is not usually decorated, but the exterior bears geometrical designs in which terraces, triangles, and parallel lines predominate. Curved lines are rare, and spirals are absent. Mugs with two handles are unrepresented. There are no ladles in the collection, but several broken handles of ladles were found in the refuse. One of these is decorated with a series of parallel, longitudinal, and transverse lines, a design as widely spread as Pueblo pottery, extending across the boundary into Mexico.

Globular Vessels.—The globular form of pottery was used for carrying water and seems to have been common at Cliff Palace. One of these vessels (pl. 25, *b*) has a small neck, and attached to it are two eyelets for insertion of the thong by which it was carried. Some of the globular vessels (pl. 25, *a*) have the neck small, the orifice wide, and the lip perforated with holes for strings. Double-lipped globular vessels, having a groove like that of a teapot, have been found in Cliff Palace as well as in other ruins of Mesa Verde and Montezuma canyon. The rims of these are generally perforated, as if for the insertion of thongs to facilitate carrying. The bottoms of these vessels are rarely concave. They are sometimes decorated on the outside, but never on the interior.

Vases.—Small vases with contracted neck and lip slightly curved, and larger vases with the same characters, occur sparingly. These (pls. 26, 27, *b*) are decorated on the exterior in geometrical designs; the interior is plain. The bases are rounded, sometimes flat, and in rare instances concave.

Disks.—Among pottery objects should be mentioned certain disks, some large, others small, some perforated in the middle, others imperforate. Several are decorated. These disks served as covers for bowls, and similar disks were employed as counters in games or as spindle whorls. None of the clay disks from Cliff Palace has a central knob or handle like those from Spruce-tree House.

Relations as determined by Pottery

In the report on Spruce-tree House, using pottery as a basis, the prehistoric culture of the Southwest, including the Gila-Salt area, which can not strictly be designated Pueblo, has been provisionally divided into several subcultural areas. Among these are the Hopi, a specialized modification of the Little Colorado, the Little Colorado proper, the San Juan, and the Gila-Salt areas.

Cliff Palace pottery symbols are not closely related to those on old Hopi ware, as typified by the collections from Sikyatki.[71] Neither Cliff Palace nor Spruce-tree

[71] Sikyatki ware is more closely related to that of the ancient Jemez and Pajarito subarea than to that made by the Snake clans when they lived at Tokónabi, their old home, or at Black Falls shortly before they arrived at Walpi. Careful study of ancient Walpi pottery made by the Bear clan before the arrival of the Snake clans shows great similarity to Sikyatki pottery, and the same holds regarding the ware from old Shongopovi.

House pottery is closely allied to that of the Little Colorado, as exemplified by Homolobi ware, but both have a closer likeness to that from Wukóki, a settlement ascribed to the Snake clans, situated near Black Falls, not far from Flagstaff, Arizona. As a rule the symbolism on pottery from the Little Colorado, which includes that of its upper tributaries, as the Zuñi, Puerco, Leroux, and Cottonwood washes, is a mixture of all types. This river valley has exerted a distributing influence in Pueblo migrations, and in its ruins are found symbols characteristic of many clans, some of which, following up the tributaries of the Salt and the Gila, have brought Casas Grandes decorative elements; others, with sources in the northeast, have contributed designs from an opposite direction. The predominating directions of ceramic culture migration in this valley have been from south to north and from west to east.[72]

The relation of Cliff Palace pottery designs to the symbolism or decorative motives characteristic of the Gila valley ruins is remote. Several geometrical patterns are common to all areas of the Southwest, but specialized features characterize each of these areas. The pottery from Cliff Palace finds its nearest relation throughout the upper San Juan region; the most distant to that of ruins in northern Arizona near Colorado Grande.[73]

Symbols on Pottery

The symbols on the Cliff Palace pottery are reducible to rectangular geometrical figures; life forms, with the rare exceptions noted above, are not represented, and the exceptional examples are crude. Contrast this condition with the pottery from Sikyatki, where three-fourths of the decorations are life designs, as figures of men or animals, many of which are highly symbolic. The "sky band" with hanging bird design, peculiar to old Hopi ware, was unknown to Cliff Palace potters. Encircling lines are unbroken, no specimen being found with the break so common to the pottery from the Hopi, Little Colorado, Gila, and Jemez subareas. The designs on food bowls are often accompanied with marginal dots. No example of the conventionalized "breath-feather" so common in Sikyatki pottery decoration occurs. Spattering with color was not practiced.

An analysis of the pottery decorations shows that the dominant forms may be reduced to a few types, of which the terrace, the spiral, the triangle, and the cross in its various forms are the most common.

Various forms and sizes of triangles, singly or in combination, constitute one of the most constant devices used by the cliff-dwellers of the Mesa Verde in the decoration of their pottery. It is common to find two series of triangles arranged

[72] In the ruins found on the banks of the Little Colorado at Black Falls, the predominating influence, as shown by pottery symbols, has been from the north. It is known from legends that Wukóki was settled by clans from the north, the close likeness to the symbols of the San Juan valley supporting traditions still current at Walpi.

[73] A thorough comparative study of Pueblo pottery symbolism is much restricted on account of lack of material from all ceramic culture areas of the Southwest. It is likewise made difficult by a mixture of types produced by the migration of clans from one area to another. The subject is capable of scientific treatment, but at present is most difficult of analysis.

on parallel lines. When the component triangles are right-angled they sometimes alternate with each other, forming a zigzag which may be sinistral or dextral. This design may be called an alternate right-angular figure.

If instead of two parallel series of right-angle triangles there are isosceles triangles, they may be known as alternate isosceles triangles. These triangles, when opposite, form a series of hour-glass figures or squares. This form is commonly accompanied by a row of dots, affixed to top and base, known as the dotted square or hour-glass figure. Hour-glass designs are commonly represented upright, but the angles of the triangles may be so placed that the series is horizontal, forming a continuous chain. Often the bases of these serially arrayed hour-glass figures are separated by rows of dots or by blank spaces.

A row of triangles, each so placed that the angles touch the middles of the sides of others in the same series, form an arc called linear triangles. The St. Andrews cross, which occurs sparingly on Mesa Verde pottery, is formed by joining the vertical angles of four isosceles triangles.

The cross and the various forms of the familiar swastika also occur on Cliff Palace pottery. The star symbol, made up of four squares so arranged as to leave a space in the middle, is yet to be found in Mesa Verde. Parallel curved lines, crooked at the end or combined with triangles and squares, occur commonly in the pottery decoration of Cliff Palace. S-shaped figures are known. Rectangles or triangles with dots, or even a line of dots alone, are not rare in the decoration. No designs representing leaves or flowers occur on pottery from Cliff Palace, nor has the spider-web pattern been found. The most common geometrical decorations are the stepped or terraced figures, generally called rain-clouds.

Pottery Rests

Among the objects found in the refuse heaps of Cliff Palace are rings, about 6 inches in diameter, woven of corn husks or cedar bark bound together with fiber of yucca or other plants. These rings (pl. 28) were evidently used as supports for earthenware vases, the bases of which are generally rounded, so that otherwise they would not stand upright. Similar rings may have been used by the women in carrying jars of water on their heads,[74] as among the Zuñi of to-day. Some of these rings may have been used in what is called the "ring and dart" game, which is often ceremonial in nature. The best made of all these objects, found by Mr. Fuller on his visit to a neighboring canyon, is shown in the accompanying illustration (pl. 28, *b*). The specimen is made of tightly woven corn husks, around which the fiber is gathered so as to form an equatorial ridge rarely present in these objects.

BASKETRY

A few instructive specimens of basketry or wicker ware were exhumed at Cliff Palace. One of the most interesting of these is the unfinished plaque shown in the accompanying figure 2.

---

[74] The Hopi use large clay canteens for this purpose, no vessels resembling which, whole or in fragments, have been found at Cliff Palace.

One specimen of basketry (pl. 29) has the form of a hopper; its whole central part was purposely omitted, but the basket is finished on the inner and outer margins. It recalls a basket used by the Ute and other Shoshonean Indians, but it is different in form from any figured in Nordenskiöld's work, and, so far as the author is acquainted with other specimens of basketry from Mesa Verde ruins, is unique. It is supposed that when used this hopper was placed on a flat or rounded stone and that corn or other seeds to be pounded were placed in it, the stone thus forming the surface upon which the seeds were treated, and the sides of the basket serving to retain the meal.

SANDALS

The sandals found at Cliff Palace (pls. 30-32) are practically the same in form, material, and weave as those recorded from Spruce-tree House. The shape of these, however, is particularly instructive, as it appears to shed light on the meaning of certain flat stones, rare in cliff-dwellings, called "sandal lasts." These stones, one of which is figured in the report on Spruce-tree House, are rectangular, flat, thin, smooth, with rounded corners, and sometimes have a notch in the rim at one end. The exceptionally formed sandal from Cliff Palace (pl. 32) is similar in shape and has a notch identical with that of the problematical stone objects, supporting the theory that the latter were used as sandal lasts, as interpreted by several authors.

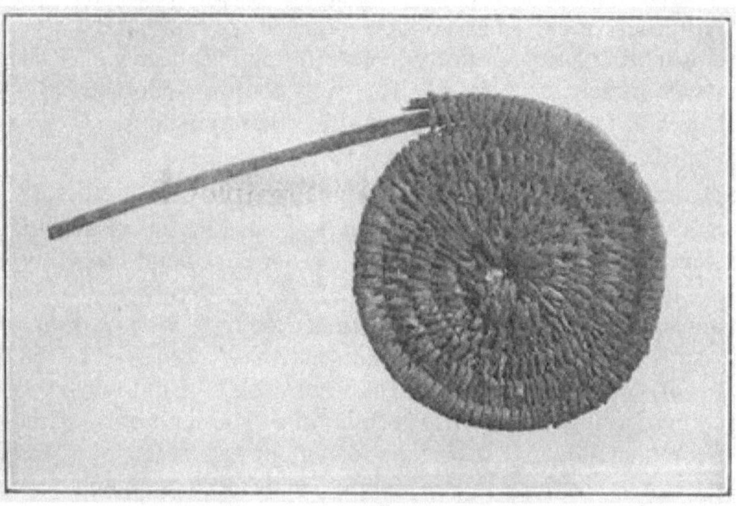

FIG. 2.—COIL OF BASKET PLAQUE.

The sandals are ordinarily made of plaited yucca leaves, their upper side being sometimes covered with corn leaves for protection of the feet. The thongs that passed between the toes are made either of yucca or other vegetable fiber, or of hide.

PLATE 33

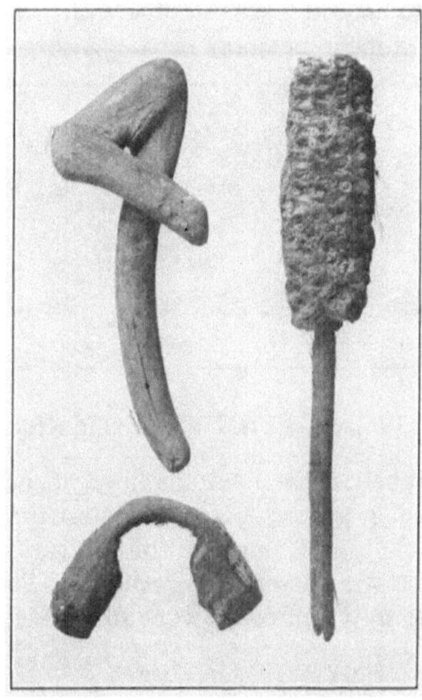

a. Billet   *b.* Objects used in game   *c.* Billet

WOODEN OBJECTS

WOODEN OBJECTS

There are several objects made of wood in the collection from Cliff Palace, some of the least problematical of which are long, pointed rods (fig. 3) with which the ancients probably made the holes in which they planted corn, in much the same way as the Hopi plant at the present day. These implements are commonly pointed at the end, but one or two are broadened and flattened. No example of the spatular variety of dibble found by others, and none showing the point of attachment of a flat stone blade, occurs in the collection. One or two short broken sticks, having a knob cut on the unbroken end, are interpreted as handles of weapons—a use that is not definitely proven. There are several sticks that evidently were used for barring windows or for holding stone door-closes in place.

Among problematical wooden objects may be mentioned billets (pl. 33), flattened on one side and rounded at each end. Two of these were found, with calcined human bones, in the inclosure used for cremation of the dead, situated at the northern end of the large refuse heap. These, like the bowls with which they were associated, were coated with a white salt-like deposit. None of the many wooden objects figured by Nordenskiöld are exactly the same as those above mentioned, although the one shown in his plate XLIII, figure 17, is very close in form and size.

Several bent twigs or loops of flexible wood from the refuse heaps were found; these are supposed to have been inserted in the masonry, one on each side of door and window openings, to hold in place the stick which served as a bolt for fastening the door or window stone in position.

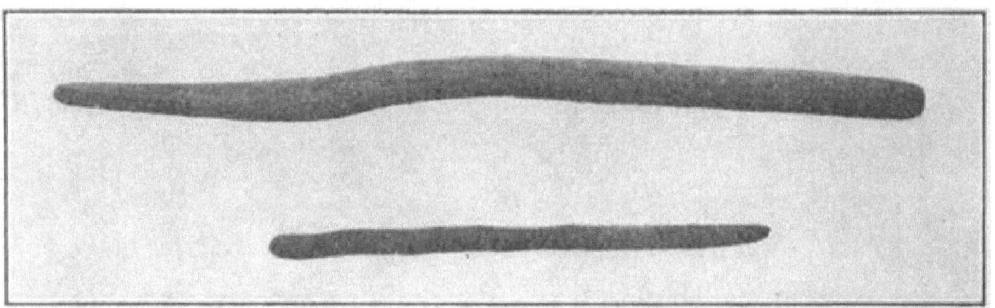

FIG. 3.—PLANTING STICKS.

Bent sticks, of dumb-bell shape, having a knob at each end (pl. 33, *b*), are believed to have been used in games. A similar object from the Mancos region is figured by Mr. Stewart Culin in his account of the games of the cliff-dwellers.[75] The ancient people of the semi-deserts of Atacama, in South America, employed a similar but larger stick, to which cords were attached for strapping bundles on their beasts of burden.

DRILLS

A small pointed stone attached with fiber to the end of a stick, similar to those found by Nordenskiöld in ruin 9 and at Long House, was found.

The Cliff Palace people kindled fire by means of the fire-drill and fire-stick (hearth), a specimen of which, similar to one collected at Spruce-tree House, is contained in the collection. Both of these fire-making implements were broken when found, apparently thrown away on that account either by the original people or by subsequent visitors.

BONE IMPLEMENTS

Many bone implements (pl. 34, 35) were found during the excavation of Cliff Palace. They are of the bones of birds and small mammals, or, now and then, of those of antelope or bear, the latter furnishing the best material for large scrapers. These implements were evidently sharpened by rubbing on the stones of walls or on the face of the cliff, as grooves, apparently made in this way, are there visible in several places. Scratches made in shaping or sharpening bones, repeatedly found on the masonry of Cliff Palace, are not peculiar, resembling those referred to in the report on Spruce-tree House. A small tube with a hole midway of its length doubtless served as a whistle, similar instruments being still often used in Hopi ceremonies to imitate the calls of birds.

Sections of bones were found tied in pairs, and while it is not clear that these

[75] *Twenty-fourth Annual Report of the Bureau of American Ethnology.*

were threaded on a cord and worn as necklaces or armlets, as Nordenskiöld suggests, they may have been tied side by side, forming a kind of breastplate not unlike that used by the Plains tribes. In a room of Spruce-tree House, according to Nordenskiöld, eight similar pieces of bone were found strung on a fine thong of tide.

Among other bone objects there is one, of unknown use, about an inch long and one-fourth of an inch in diameter, nearly cylindrical in shape. A bone with a hole in one end, similar to those figured by Nordenskiöld, forms part of the collection.

PLATE 34

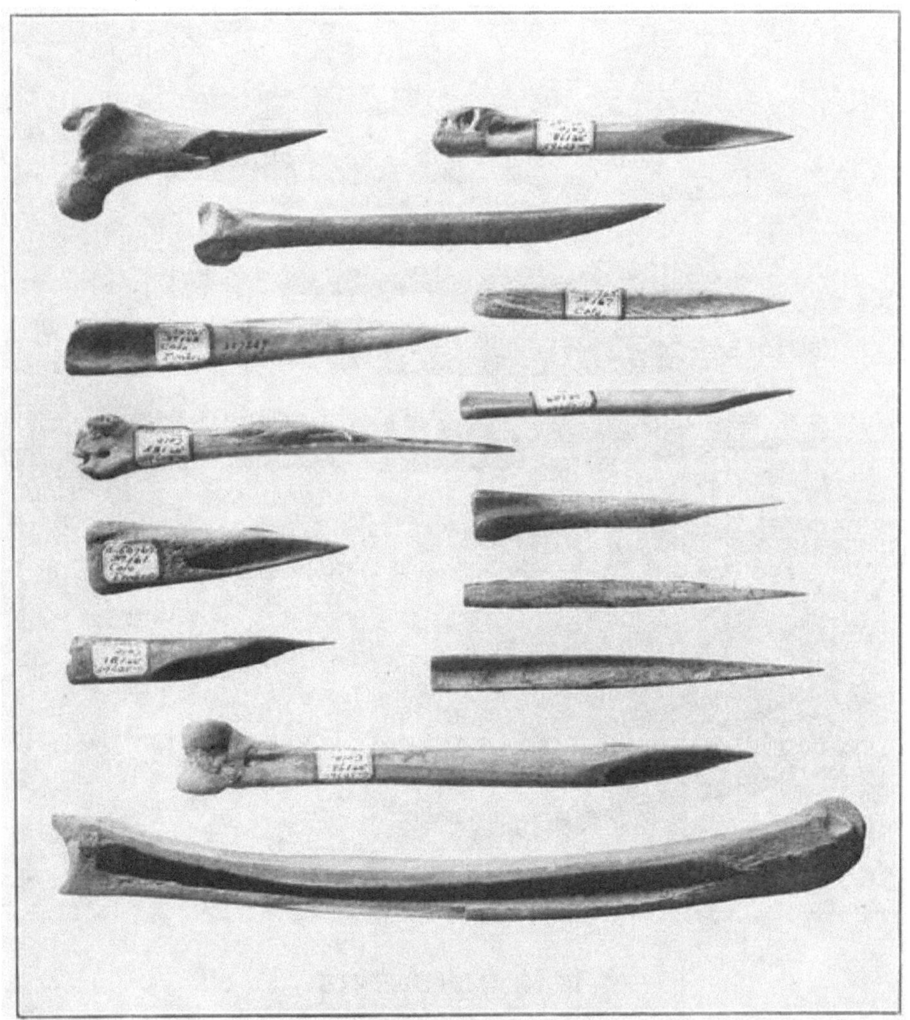

BONE IMPLEMENTS

PLATE 35

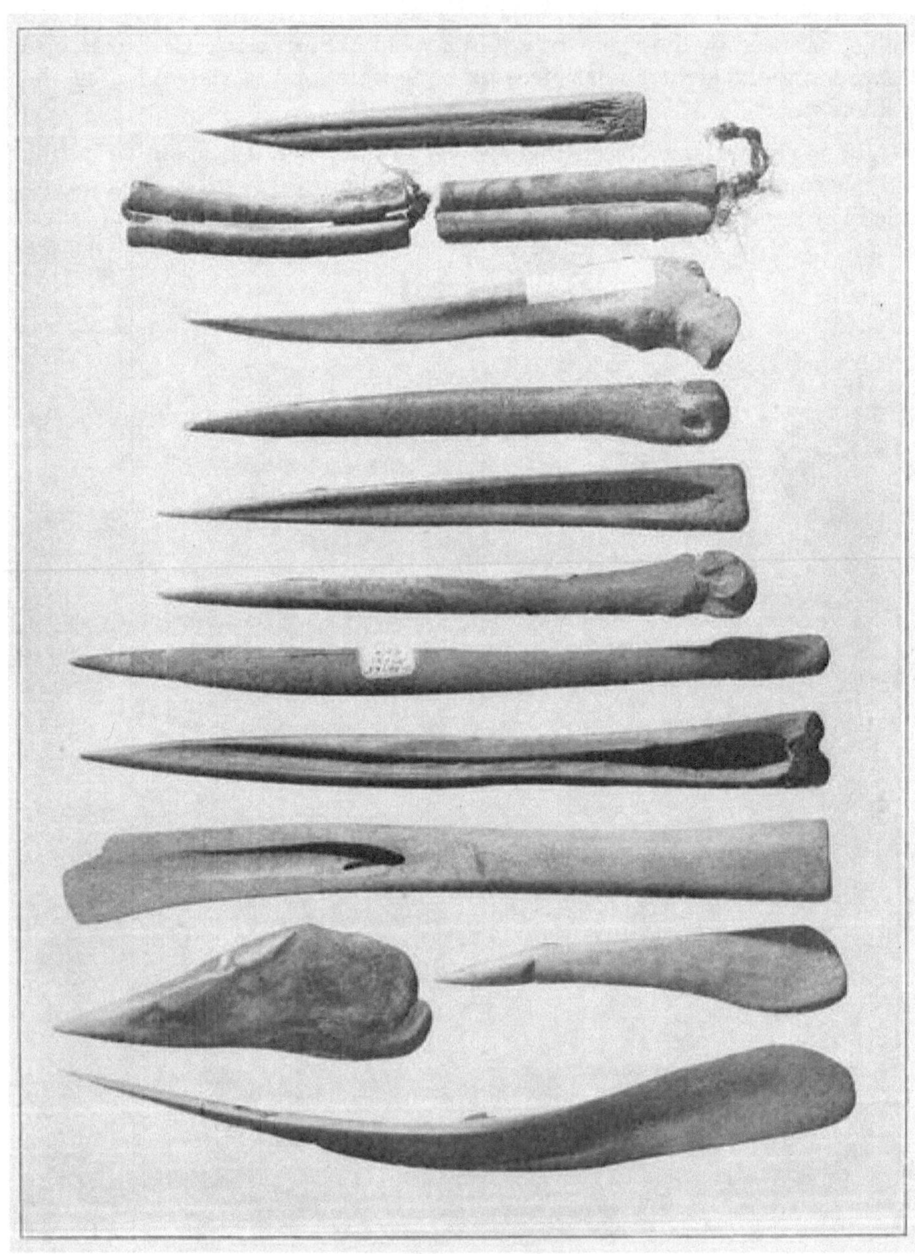

BONE IMPLEMENTS

TURQUOISE EAR PENDANTS AND OTHER OBJECTS

The single specimen of turquoise found at Cliff Palace was probably an ear pendant, and a black jet bead was apparently used for the same purpose. With the polished cylinder of hematite found one can still paint the face or body a reddish color, as the Hopi do with a similar object. From the sipapû of kiva D there was taken a small deerskin bag, tied with yucca fiber and containing a material resembling iron pyrites, evidently an offering of some kind to the gods of the underworld.

A button made of lignite, and beads of the same material, were found in the refuse heap in front of the ruin after a heavy rain. The former is broken, but it resembles that found at Spruce-tree House, although it is not so finely made, and also one from Homólobi, a ruin on the Little Colorado, near Winslow, Arizona.

SEEDS

The cobs and seeds of corn, squash and pumpkin seeds, beans, and fragments of gourds give some idea of the vegetable products known to the Cliff Palace people. Corn furnished the most important food of the people, and its dried leaves, stalks, and tassels were abundant in all parts of their refuse heaps. Naturally, in a cave where many small rodents have lived for years, it is rare to find seed corn above ground that has not been appropriated by these animals, and in the dry, alkaline bone-phosphate dust edible corn is not very common, although now and then occurs a cob; with attached seeds. The corn of Cliff Palace, already figured by Nordenskiöld, resembles that still cultivated by some of the Hopi.

TEXTILES

The Cliff Palace people manufactured fairly good cloth, the component cords or strings being of two or three strands and well twisted. So finely made and durable are some of these cords that they might be mistaken for white men's work; some of them, however, are very coarse, and are tied in hanks. Among varieties of cords, may be mentioned those wound with feathers, from which textiles, ordinarily called "feather cloth," was made. Yucca and cotton were employed in the manufacture of almost all kinds of fabrics. A few fragments of netting were found.

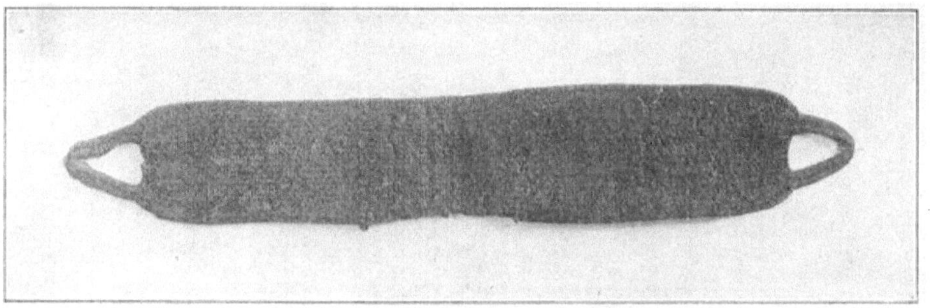

FIG. 4.—WOVEN FOREHEAD BAND.

The finest cloth was manufactured from cotton, a good specimen, of which, showing a pattern woven in different colors, is contained in the collection.

Several woven belts, and also a head-band similar to that figured in the report on Spruce-tree House, were uncovered by the excavations.

The largest fragment of cloth was taken out of the crematory, or inclosure containing the calcined human bones, at the northern end of the larger refuse heap. It appears to have been a portion of a bag, or possibly of a head covering, but it is so fragmentary that its true use is unknown. The pattern is woven in darker colored threads, with a selvage at two ends. The material out of which it was made has not been definitely determined, but it closely resembles that of the specimen figured by Nordenskiöld (plate L) from Mug House. Our excavations were rewarded with a fine woven head-band with loops at the ends (fig. 4), similar to that described and figured in the report on Spruce-tree House. Several small fragments of cloth were recovered from the refuse heap, but none of them was large enough to indicate the form of the garment to which they originally belonged.

In the group of fabrics may be included nets and cloth with feathers wound around warp and woof, similar to those figured from Spruce-tree House.

There were several specimens of yucca strings, tied in loops, generally six in number, which presumably were devoted to the same purpose as by the present Hopi, who attach to the string six ears of corn, representing the cardinal points on the six-directions altar, and hang them on the walls of a priest's house. If the cliff-dwellers used this string for a similar purpose, it would appear that they, like the Hopi, recognized six cardinal points—north, west, south, east, above, and below—and worshiped gods of these directions, to which they erected altars.[76]

---

[76] For a Hopi six-directions altar, see *Journal of American Ethnology and Archæology*, Vol. II, 1892.

HUMAN BURIALS

As has been seen, there were two methods of disposing of the dead—by inhumation and by cremation. The former may have been either house burial or burial in the refuse heaps in the rear of the buildings. With both forms of disposing of the dead mortuary food offerings were found. Evidences of prehistoric burials and cremation were found both on the mesa above Cliff Palace and in the ruin.[77]

The practice of cremation among the cliff-dwellers has long been known. Nordenskiöld writes (p. 49):

That cremation, however, was sometimes practiced by the Cliff Dwellers seems probable from the fact that Richard Wetherill observed in the same ruin, when the above-mentioned burial chamber was found, bodies which had apparently been burnt, together with the pottery belonging to the dead.

The evidences of cremation found in the inclosure at the northern end of the refuse space of Cliff Palace is conclusive. The calcined bones uncovered here were also accompanied with mortuary pottery, cloth, and wooden objects.

The flexed position of the bodies of the dead occurs constantly in the earth burials, which may be explained by the almost universal belief among primitive people that when the body is returned to "mother earth" it should be placed in the posture it normally had before birth. In house burials at Spruce-tree House the bodies were sometimes extended at full length, which may be interpreted to mean that the dead were not returned to the earth mother. There was no uniformity of posture in the burials at Cliff Palace.

The work at Cliff Palace was undertaken at too late a day to recover any mummified human remains, all having been previously removed. Nordenskiöld's figures and descriptions of desiccated human bodies from other Mesa Verde cliff-dwellings would apply, in a measure, to those from Cliff Palace.

---

[77] The house burials appear to have been mainly those of priests or other important personages.

CONCLUSIONS

While the work of excavation and repair of Cliff Palace described in the preceding pages adds nothing distinctly new to existing knowledge of cliff-dweller culture, it renders a more comprehensive idea of the conditions of life in one of the largest of these interesting ancient settlements in our Southwest. Of all the questions that present themselves after a work of this kind, perhaps the most important, from a scientific point of view, is, What relation exists between the culture of Cliff Palace and that of the neighboring pueblos? Directly across the canyon, in full view of Cliff Palace, there is a typical pueblo ruin, almost identical in character with many others scattered throughout the Southwest, some of which are known to have been inhabited in historic times by ancestors of Pueblo peoples still living. The contribution here made to the knowledge of cliff-dwelling culture will, it is hoped, shed light on the question, In what way are the cliff-dwellers and the Pueblos related?

The relationship in culture of the former people of Cliff Palace to those of the large pueblo ruin on the mesa across the canyon is most instructive. How were the inhabitants of these two settlements related; and were the two sites inhabited simultaneously, or is the pueblo ruin older than Cliff Palace? So far as the culture of the inhabitants of the two is known (and knowledge of the pueblo is scant), the two settlements were synchronously inhabited, but nothing in them gives indication of the period of their occupancy. These questions can be settled only by the excavation of this pueblo or of some similar ruin on the plateau.[78] Nordenskiöld, with the data possessed by him, did not hesitate to express decided views on this point:

> We are forced to conclude that they [cliff-houses] were abandoned later than the villages on the mesa. Some features, for example, the superposition of walls constructed with the greatest proficiency on others built in a more primitive fashion (see plate XIII) indicate that the cliff-dwellings have been inhabited at two different periods. They were first abandoned, and had partly fall-

[78] A true comparison of the mesa habitation and the cliff-dwelling can be made only by renewed work on the former, which is now little more than a huge pile of fallen walls. Present indications show a greater antiquity of the mesa ruin, the site of which afforded more adequate protection. On this supposition the mesa ruins would be considered older than the cliff ruins, and those of the valley the most ancient. If the ruins in Montezuma valley are the oldest, we can not suppose that the culture originated in the cliffs and spread to the valley. The circular subterranean kiva bears indication of having originated in valleys rather than in caverns. Nordenskiöld does not mention the large ruin on the bluff west of Cliff Palace.

en into ruin, but were subsequently repeopled, new walls being now erected on the ruins of the old. The best explanation hereof seems to be the following: On the plateaux and in the valleys the Pueblo tribes attained their widest distribution and their highest development. The numerous villages at no great distance from each other were strong enough to defy their hostile neighbors. But afterwards, from causes difficult of elucidation, a period of decay set in, the number and population of the villages gradually decreased, and the inhabitants were again compelled to take refuge in the remote fastnesses. Here the people of the Mesa Verde finally succumbed to their enemies. The memory of their last struggle is preserved by the numerous human bones found in many places, strewn among the ruined cliff-dwellings. These human remains occur in situations where it is impossible to assume that they have been interred.

Closely connected with the relative age and the identity of the Mesa Verde cliff-house and pueblo culture are the age and relationship of different cliff-houses of the same region, for example, Cliff Palace and Spruce-tree House. The relative number of kivas may shed light on this point.

The relative proportion of the number of kivas to secular houses varies in Cliff Palace and Spruce-tree House. In the former there are about 7 secular rooms to every kiva; in the latter about 15. Long House has a still more marked difference, there being here only a few secular houses and a maximum number of kivas. Whether this variation has any meaning it is impossible to say definitely; theoretically, as compared with modern pueblos, the proportionately larger number of kivas points to a sociological condition in Cliff Palace characteristic of more primitive times. The larger the number of kivas relatively to secular rooms the older the ruin. Long House would be regarded as older than Cliff Palace, and Cliff Palace older than Spruce-tree House, Balcony House being the most modern and the last of the four to be deserted. A cliff-dwelling with a kiva but without secular rooms is rare, and one with secular rooms but without kivas is likewise unusual. Where the latter exists it is so situated as to indicate that it was subordinated to neighboring large cliff-dwellings.

The relative number of circular kivas in ruins and in modern inhabited pueblos where the circular form of room is found is larger in the ruins than in the inhabited pueblos. The proportionate number of circular rooms to secular rooms in cliff-dwellings of the Mesa Verde is also larger than in pueblo ruins like those of the Chaco. Apparently the older the pueblo the greater the relative number of kivas. If, as is suspected, a larger number of kivas indicates relatively greater age, the explanation may be sought in the amalgamation of clans and the development of religious fraternities. Hypothetically, in early days each clan had its own men's room, or kiva, but when clans were united by marriage and secret ceremonies were no longer limited to individual clans, the participants belonging to several clans, a religious fraternity was developed and several clan kivas consolidated or were enlarged into fraternity kivas such as we find among the Hopi and other Pueblos.

From a study of kivas the conclusion is that Spruce-tree House is more modern than Cliff Palace. This conclusion is borne out also by the fact that the water supply at Spruce-tree House is more abundant than that at Cliff Palace.

In one or two architectural features Cliff Palace is unique, although sharing with other cliff-houses of the Mesa Verde National Park many minor characters. The first difference between Cliff Palace and Spruce-tree House, outside of the disparity in their size and the relatively large proportion of secular to ceremonial rooms in the latter, is the existence in the former of terraces and retaining walls. Spruce-tree House is built on one level, above which rise the secular houses while below are the ceremonial rooms or kivas. The contrast of this simple condition with that of Cliff Palace, with its three terraces and the complicated front wall at several levels thereby necessitated, is apparent.

There are several other ruins in the Mesa Verde Park in which the configuration of the rear of the cave led to the construction of the cliff-house in terrace form. This is well exemplified in the Spring House, where buildings on an upper level occupy much the same relation to those below as the ledge houses to the main ruin, and in ruins in the Canyon de Chelly, like those in Mummy Cave, where this relation of the buildings on the ledge to those on top of the talus is even more pronounced. Architectural features in cliff-houses are due to the geological structure of the cave in which they are situated rather than to cultural differences.

Nothing was found to indicate that Cliff Palace was inhabited during the historic period. The inhabitants were not acquainted with metals brought by white men to the Southwest. The absence of glass and of glazed pottery is also significant. No sheep, horses, or other beasts of burden paid them tribute. In fact, there is no evidence that they had ever heard of white men. These ruins belong to the stone age in America and show no evidence of white man's culture.

Except that it is prehistoric, the period at which Cliff Palace was inhabited is therefore largely a matter for archeological investigation to determine, and thus far no decisive evidence bearing on that point has been produced. It has been held that Cliff Palace is five hundred years old, and some writers have added five centuries to this guess; but the nature of the evidence on which this extreme antiquity is ascribed to the ruin is not warranted by the evidence available.

No additional information was obtained bearing on current theories of the causes that led the ancient occupants of the Mesa Verde cliff-dwellings to adopt this inhospitable and inconvenient habitat. It is probable that one and the same cause led to the abandonment of Spruce-tree House, Cliff Palace, and other Mesa Verde cliff-houses. The inhabitants of these buildings struggled to gain a livelihood against their unfavorable environment until a too-exacting nature finally overcame them. There are no indications that the abandonment of Cliff Palace was cataclysmic in nature: it seems to have been a gradual desertion by one clan after another. One of the primary reasons was change of climate, which caused the water supply to diminish and the crops to fail; but long before its final desertion many clans abandoned the place, and drifting from point to point sought home-sites where water was more abundant. All available data lend weight to a belief that the cliff-houses of Mesa Verde were not abandoned simultaneously, but were deserted one by one. Possibly the inhabitants retired to the river valleys, where water was constant, and later gave up life on the mesa. But even then the culture was not allowed to continue unmodified by outside influences. Where the descendants of Cliff Palace now dwell, or whether they are now extinct, can be determined only by additional research.

Evidence is rapidly accumulating in support of the theory that the "cliff-dweller culture" of our Southwest was preceded by a "pit-house culture," the most prominent feature of which is the small circular or rectangular rooms, artificially excavated laterally in cliffs or vertical in the ground, which served this ancient people either as dwellings or for storage. The side walls of these rooms were supported in some instances by upright logs, and commonly clay was plastered directly on the walls of the excavations. The architectural survival of subterranean rooms exists among the cliff-dwellings in circular underground kivas, the variations of which are so well illustrated in Cliff Palace.

In connection with these "pit rooms," which are never large, may be mentioned the large subterranean artificial excavations found scattered over the Pueblo area of the Southwest. Such occur in the Gila valley, and have been reported from the San Juan drainage; they have been identified as reservoirs and also as kivas. Some of these subterranean rooms are rightly identified as kivas, but others have architectural features that render this interpretation improbable. What their function was and how they are connected with the people who built the smaller subterranean rooms of the Southwest can be determined only by excavations and a study of the features of both types.

The most important step that remains to be taken in the scientific study of the ruins of the Mesa Verde National Park is to discover the relation of the culture of Cliff Palace to that of the neighboring pueblo. This will necessitate the scientific excavation and repair of the latter ruin and a comparison of its major and minor antiquities with those of Cliff Palace. The age of cliff-dwellings in different parts of the Southwest undoubtedly varies. Certain Pueblo ruins are older than some cliff-dwellings, and there are cliff-houses more ancient than Pueblo ruins. Continued research in the Mesa Verde region will doubtless shed light on the relative age of Cliff Palace and the great pueblo ruin opposite it.

Lector House believes that a society develops through a two-fold approach of continuous learning and adaptation, which is derived from the study of classic literary works spread across the historic timeline of literature records. Therefore, we aim at reviving, repairing and redeveloping all those inaccessible or damaged but historically as well as culturally important literature across subjects so that the future generations may have an opportunity to study and learn from past works to embark upon a journey of creating a better future.

This book is a result of an effort made by Lector House towards making a contribution to the preservation and repair of original ancient works which might hold historical significance to the approach of continuous learning across subjects.

HAPPY READING & LEARNING!

LECTOR HOUSE LLP
E-MAIL: lectorpublishing@gmail.com